WOGAN'S
TWELVE

WOGAN'S TWELVE

Terry Wogan

First published in Great Britain in 2007 by
Orion Books
an imprint of the Orion Publishing Group Ltd
Orion House, 5 Upper St Martin's Lane,
London WC2H 9EA
An Hachette Livre UK Company

3 5 7 9 10 8 6 4

A CIP catalogue record for this book is available
from the British Library.

ISBN 978 0 7528 8843 9 (hardback)
ISBN: 978 0 7528 9144 6 (Airport Trade Paperback)

Printed in Great Britain by Clays Ltd, St Ives plc

The Orion Publishing Group's policy is to use papers
that are natural, renewable and recyclable and made from wood
grown in sustainable forests. The logging and manufacturing
processes are expected to conform to the environmental
regulations of the country of origin.

Every effort has been made to fulfil requirements with
regard to reproducing copyright material. The author and publisher
will be glad to rectify any omissions at the earliest opportunity.

All cartoons courtesy of Matt Pritchett.

www.orionbooks.co.uk

To the usual suspects, without whose love, encouragement and inspiration, I'd be lounging on a beach somewhere, drinking a cocktail and planning my dinner. Thanks, folks!

Let's hear it again for Mark and Luigi, Amanda, Ian and Clare, my loyal and beloved TOGs, the greatest and funniest cartoonist of the age, Matt Pritchett, and particularly those poor unfortunates who had to decipher my handwriting.

Intro to Diary

This homely record of a year gone forever should really have started in July, but I lost my notes, and as anybody of my vintage will attest, it's hard to remember what happened yesterday, so trying to cast what remains of my mind back a whole month is asking for the moon.

So, friends, it's a shotgun start at August 2006. Here, let me take your hand as we dawdle into a world that was. Take your seats – fasten your seat belts – we have lift-off . . .

MATT

9 August 2006

'Marketing' is now at the very heart of the BBC, which accounts for the fruitless pursuit of the Phantom Viewer – the young male, sixteen to twenty-three, whose attention and spending power all advertising agencies crave. The sad fact that the young male in question would rather be in the pub, the disco, the rave, on Xbox, eBay, YouTube or chilling out with the young babe of his choice – anything rather than watch television – is driving marketing, and the sixth floor of Television Centre bananas. No use telling them that their 'core' audience – parents, young families, the middle-aged and the elderly – are sitting patiently there in front of the box, waiting to be entertained . . .

The news today that the BBC has appointed a Head of Diversity brings the blood rushing to the head. Another new Beeb buzzword, when we've only just got a handle on 'compliance'. And what happened to 'cut the crap'?

Years ago, BBC producers used to jest about a mythical figure, the 'PPO' – Programmes Preventions Officer. With Diversity, Compliance, Talent and at least two different controllers (Programmes and Commissioning) per network, nobody's laughing now . . .

Naturally, the listener could not be left out of it:

Tel,

I am very glad that my sister has made such a big impact at Radio 2, it's only been 3 months since she started there as a cleaner. If you bump into Di as she is mopping out the bogs

on the fourth floor say hello from me and tell her her family
are so proud.
Love,
Una
PS Is Deadly's office still the 3rd trap on the left?

UNA VERSITY

10 August 2006

I suppose people have always been fascinated by their forebears, but programmes like *Who Do You Think You Are?* have whipped enthusiasm for delving into the upper branches of family trees into a fine old frenzy. I've just come across a magazine where, unbidden – at least by me – a genealogist has researched the proud family Wogan. I don't know where some people dig up their ancient information, but in the preamble to his painstaking digging, this fellow referred to my 'writing the lyrics of "The Floral Dance"', and to the TV chat show where I was 'walloped by Grace Jones'. Since the words of 'The Floral Dance' were written before I was born, and it was the late lamented Russell Harty who got the Grace Jones slap across the chops, you won't mind if I take genealogy with a grain of salt from now on.

12 August 2006

It's hard not to be moved at the new, exciting face of television news. Nothing to do with Natasha, Fiona, Sophie or even

George. It's the endless variations that have been added by a thinking newsroom. 'Let's not sit on our laurels,' cries the editor. So, the readers stand. Then they sit down, bringing it all to a nail-biting climax by standing up again. Then, blow me down if they don't sit again for the big finish. Creative broadcasting at its best, combining thought, flair and pace, with a frisson of the unexpected. What are they going to do next – sit or stand? It makes such a difference to the boring old news. As I sat in my customary trance before the microphone, I thought what a difference it would make if radio newsreaders would get up and move about a bit, like Tony Hancock's mother's gravy, but old habits die hard on the wireless. I asked a BBC2 newsreader if he favoured standing or sitting while intoning the bulletin. 'Lying down, actually,' he replied languidly, flicking an imaginary speck of dust from his irreproachable cuff. And yet, can television news ever compare with the great moments of radio news? Only this week, I heard a Radio 4 newsreader, having delivered a polished, flawless performance, pause, and then say: 'Ah! That was yesterday's bulletin, I'm afraid . . .'

Reading the news

15 August 2006

The latest indication of rampant insanity in high places is the idea put forward today that roads should be constructed only after first taking into consideration the lot of the butterfly. You'd want to be hard of heart not to love the delicate creature, but one of the more notable features of the butterfly is its ability to fly. So, if naughty old road-building is disturbing their habitat, unlike us leaden-footed, earth-bound mortals, they simply flap their little wings, and off they fly to another, less stressful environment.

I have my own suspicions that the people behind this tosh are the same ones who last year were asking motorists to count the dead insects on their windscreens, because the little birds were not getting enough to eat. So have a care before you start the engine of your petrol-guzzling, carbon-spouting monster! It will lead to more dead insects, starving birds and some very inconvenienced butterflies.

Naturally, Dame Fran Godfrey, newsreader, traffic reporter and right old softy who feeds pigeons in her window-box, fussed like Rebecca of Sunnybrook Farm over the poor little butterflies.

> *Sweet little butterfly*
> *Just watch it flutter by*
> *Giving dear Frances much cheer.*
> *But nasty road planners*
> *Forgetting good manners*
> *Are making its home disappear.*

Lepidoptera on the wing
Make Fran's day start to zing.
With a handbook to cast out her woes.
Designers of carriageways
Now have to mend their ways.
Or with Godfrey they'll soon come to blows.

THE CROOKED MAN OF
OLD BANGOR TOWN

16 August 2006

How did we get on to the subject of 'bloaters' this morning? It's all coming back: June Brown, aka Dot Cotton on *EastEnders*, last night made bloater sandwiches for her husband Jim Brannan's little nieces, and I expressed the pardonable doubt that such a thing as bloater paste still existed. Surely it was a staple of the hungry rationing years after the last unpleasantness, lost in the mists of time, along with Snoek, Spam fritters and dripping? Anyway, says I, who should know better what a bloater is? I got my answer:

A bloater is a straw hat. Some of the bigger boys used to wear them at my school back in the 60s. Small boys didn't as their bloaters usually got stamped upon.

PETER PENNINGTON

A big thank you to Fran and yourself for explaining what a bloater is. Why then, did Harold Lloyd, Maurice Chevalier and Frankie Vaughan use to wear one on their heads? I

*believe little Elty John also plonks one on his head now and
again, perhaps you could ask him the reason!*
   Regards,

RALPHY

Has nobody got a sensible word to say?

*Bloater is herring first developed at Yarmouth in 1835.
Bloaters that are prepared whole are said to owe their special
flavour to the activity of gut enzymes. The fish are dry-salted
for about 12 hours, washed to remove surplus salt, threaded on
metal speats, and stacked in the kiln to smoke.*

MICHAEL SPENCER

Oh. Sorry I asked . . .

17 August 2006

I knew it. The first thing to greet me in the studio this morning? A case of bloater paste . . .

Somewhere during yesterday's bloater controversy I must have let slip that my second volume of autobiography, *Mustn't Grumble*, is being published in a month's time:

*What Ho Me Old Man of Letters (that's a postman, isn't it?),
   Did I hear you mention your new book yesterday? What's it
called? 'Doesn't Mumble'? Never has a book been better titled,
say I. Your voice is stentorian, yet mellow. Like Donald
Sinden ringing a bell with his tongue, like a perfectly tuned*

8

foghorn, dipped in treacle! But what I really want to know is, are you doing a book signing tour? A bit of the old publicity? And if you are, do you need a warm-up man? Picture it: you lounging in a hammock or whatever you do, as your adoring public queues to have you sign your book, then I charge on, in my signature role of Aramis from The Three Musketeers . . . *'All For One – And I'm The One!' Then I do a few songs, comic ditties, torch songs, you name it. I have a large reper-toire, but you can't get the strings for it these days. So I won't bring it. Then I finish by doing a few death scenes from my old film noir thrillers: 'Watch out Guv', 'e's got an 'atchet!' Tell the audience, don't show them! Then if there's time, you can sign a few books, as long as you do it quietly! What do you think? Shall I get my tabard out of storage? I can be ready in the time it takes to order a cab.*

Cheery Pip,

CHUFFER DANDRIDGE

Dear Chuffer, our resident resting Shakespearian actor-manager, ever present with his racy tales of treading the boards to the roar of the greasepaint, permanently hard up in his timeless search for that elusive white fiver that Larry – or was it Johnny? – borrowed from him in the bar of Wyndham's all those years ago . . .

21 August 2006

A Monday morning like any other, and then, suddenly, I was no more. The music played, but the voice of Wogan was no longer heard in the land. Somewhere in the electronic entrails a rubber band had snapped, and Studio 6C Western House, home of BBC Radio 2, was silenced. The music, on another computer, tinkled merrily away but, from me, blessed silence. Engineers and technicians dashed purposefully around . . . Well, they stood over the offending machinery, sucked their teeth and shook their heads – the usual procedure when anything goes wrong – but could offer no solution to the crisis. Apparently, the new equipment – German, and the finest licence-fee payers' money can buy – is brilliant when it's working, but when anything goes wrong . . . The music came to an end, and while we were deciding what to do, I played the next record. More sucking of teeth, shaking of heads, but no panic, this is the BBC, and anyway nobody has a clue. The newsreader was Alan Dedicoat, for it was he, Voice of the Balls, King Deadly, the Wealdstone Weather-boy, whom fate had deployed that morning to carry the can, to be the keeper of the flame of BBC Broadcasting. So, when the next record slowly faded, he spoke up from the news studio, filling the deathly hush with his ever-berating, if somewhat nasal, tones. Meanwhile, Barrowlands Boyd and myself had gathered up the vital material – emails, letters, coffee, remains of bacon butties – and made our way to another studio as the band played on. Switch on the lights, the computers, test the microphone, stick the headphones on, and bingo! We're on the road again!

I tell the world what happened, everything's all right, Daddy's home again, God's in His heaven, little imagining the unnamed dread that had struck at the heart of the loyal listener. You'd think people would be grateful for a pause in the endless twittering that is 'Wake Up To Wogan,' but no, cock-eyed optimists to a TOG, they assumed the worst. Knowing that nothing but a monumental natural disaster could shut me up, and having noticed no volcanoes erupting nor meteorites striking the planet a glancing blow, they reasoned there could be only one other reason for a Wogan silence: the Grim Reaper had struck me in the mazzard.

TOGs assume worst

For days afterwards, strangers stopped me in streets, bars and shops to tell me that they thought I'd gone to my eternal reward. They looked at me strangely, sympathetically, as you would at someone who had barely eluded the jaws of death. I tried to assure them that it was merely a technical hiccup, and nothing to do with me, but I got the distinct impression that they thought I was covering something up. Or maybe it was just disappointment; you know, when someone who's boring you stiff leaves the room, and, even as you're breathing a sigh of relief, they come back in again. Of the many letters that the incident provoked, these will give you a flavour of public reaction to the day they shut his gob:

There I was trying to gently introduce myself to Monday morning when my husband came rushing into my sanctum and announced that the flooring man was here (one hour earlier than expected) and 'Something very serious has happened to Terry Wogan and they're just playing music!' Well . . . what to do? . . . I thought my world had ended . . . how would I go on without Wogan? . . . he's always been there?! . . . I had a cup of tea and lived the next half-hour in a daze . . . imagining what this would mean to the nation . . . Then the floor man was drilling and hammering and I was feeling as if my world had collapsed and I suddenly realised that the voice on the radio that was burbling on for the last five minutes was . . . yes . . . it was, that Irish Togmaster . . . he was there, he was alive and well!!! So . . . why couldn't someone have told me that it was his equipment that was sick not him? . . . I'm going to take a long time to get over this! I might be suing for emotional trauma . . . do you still do those T-shirts, badges, or mugs . . . that would sort it!!

TINKABELL

At eight forty-eight precisely
On Monday the twenty-first
A silence fell on the BBC
The machines had done their worst
A call went out to Deadlycoat
Who to the rescue came
And bravely stepped into the breach
To claim his moment of fame
So hail to good old Deadly
The saviour of the show
Now we don't need you any more
So go on, off you go!

WILTING

*I don't mean that Terry, in fact, you had me worried, I
thought something had happened to you, it was such a relief
to hear your voice once more . . . don't you ever do that to us
again.*

BAZ

It's extraordinary, I'd never assume that silence spelt fatality. If
I get a pain in my chest, I put it down to indigestion. I suspect
that I have a very low-level survival instinct, and I'm sure pes-
simists live longer than optimists like me. When the terrible
disaster of 9/11 happened in New York, I thought of how I
would have reacted if I had been in one of the Twin Towers on
that awful day and seen a plane crash into the other one. A pes-
simist, a survivalist, would have been out of the door, down the
stairs and into the street before the second plane struck. I'm
sure that I would have hung around on the foolish, optimistic,
non-self-preservation basis that it couldn't happen again, and
not to me . . . I'm always calm in a crisis, and one day it *will*
be the death of me . . .

22 August 2006

It's the kind of bureaucratic, politically correct nonsense that
seems to come up every second day now, and drives my otherwise kindly listeners into hissy fits: Ofcom – and I can't be
bothered to translate that – has just upheld a complaint from
a viewer that Boomerang, a children's TV channel, had shown
a cartoon of *Tom and Jerry*, depicting Tom (the cat) smoking a
roll-up cigarette.

From a bursting postbag:

Dearest Terry,

I would like to say that I find the complaints re: Tom and Jerry *to be completely ridiculous. I personally grew up on the said cartoon and consider myself perfectly normal.*

I believe that the fact that I wear baggy stockings, pink slippers, and have a strong desire to kick my no good lazy husband (who happens to be called Thomas) is totally unrelated.

AMANDA HUGANKIS

If only they'd done it when I was a lad but alas it's too late now. I refer, of course, to the timely censoring of that most influential of programmes Tom and Jerry.

For too long they have been allowed to peddle their vile trade and what is the upshot?

I'll tell you what it is, pal! 60 tabs a day and 10 cigars as well, that's what it is!

I watched these two as mere striplings, through my youth and indeed into my adulthood and I find that I can't get anything done at all as I need all my time to smoke.

And to think that it's all down to Tom and Jerry. *I knew it was somebody's fault and now the truth is out I intend to sue. Somebody will pay.*

But now if you'll forgive me I must go and suspend a grand piano from a block and tackle as I want to drop it onto my next-door neighbour because last night he chopped my head off with a rather large axe.

I think perhaps he watched Tom and Jerry *too.*

PC GONEMAD
TRUMPTON POLICE STATION

23 August 2006

All right-thinking folk will be delighted at the news that the hole in the Antarctic ozone layer is closing up. Whether this is due to a lessening in the methane gas being expelled by millions of New Zealand sheep, or the eschewing of the use of hairspray and underarm deodorant, we may never know. Of course, there will always be those who overreact:

> *Dear Sir,*
>
> *Well, what great news from the US of A, the hole in the ozone layer is beginning to close again.*
>
> *Hip Hip Hooray!*
>
> *We've been celebrating in our house already.*
>
> *I've just been out and hosed the lawn for the first time in months, the children have turned the televisions on in their rooms, to be left on all day.*
>
> *The memsahib has driven her gas-guzzling 1960s Austin Princess out of the garage and left it warming up for half an hour in the drive while she nips indoors to apply her make-up.*
>
> *Even Granny's taken up pipe smoking again.*
>
> *Ah! All is well with the world again.*
>
> *Yours,*
>
> ZEBEEDEE DOODAH

People should have a care. That's the kind of talk that could put a scientist out of work . . .

In a foolish old world where funds for vital medical research are pitifully low, it's good to see that funds are readily available for this kind of thing: 'Research shows that while a cow's vocabulary is limited to one word with but a single syllable – "Moo!", not all "moos" are the same.' I should say not – herds from the West Country have a distinct Somerset twang, Brummie moos have been heard in the Midlands, and there are even suggestions of Estuary English in the Saarf-East. How big, d'you think, is the hole in the ozone layer over Britain? I think the rays are getting to some researchers' brains . . .

24 August 2006

Some years ago – I won't say how many because I've reached the age where everything I think happened last year was at least five years ago – Helen and I decided to tour the Italian Lakes – Como, Garda, Maggiore, Lucerne on the Swiss border. The scenery was lovely, the weather fine; we found a lovely golf course above Menaggio between mountain and lake, and stayed awake all night to the town's church bells – every hour on the hour. It would have been perfect, if it hadn't been for the food and wine. I get pretty tired of people telling me how they prefer Italian food to French, and how the Italians taught the French about cooking in the first place. Well, *scusi* and all that, but I've never had a really great meal in an Italian restaurant, anywhere. On our Italian Lakes trip we tried all sorts, from simple to Michelin-starred, and the best Italian meal we had was in Switzerland, a perfect pasta with basil and tomato. I've had plenty of good Italian food in London, but nothing I would call 'great'.

Tonight, in Verona, was no exception – cheery ambience,

smiling waiters, reasonable wine, but food, a disappointment. We're staying in a quirky little place called the Gabbia D'oro, with our friends for a thousand years, Michael and Lorna Smith. They invite us to Glyndebourne for the opera, and we take them to Garsington every year. So no prizes for guessing why we're in Verona: it's *Tosca* tomorrow night, and *Madame Butterfly* the following evening. We've seen the operas several times before, but the open-air setting of the huge Roman arena in Verona promises to be something else ... So, forget the *gelati*, I'll have a sambucca. I didn't come to Italy for the food, anyway ...

25 August 2006

These are the best croissants I've ever had, but I'm not changing my mind about the food, just yet. We're in the sunshine of Verona, all beautiful squares and ancient arches, with a river running by houses that haven't changed for centuries. In a little space, hardly bigger than an alcove, is the balcony under which Romeo wooed Juliet. In such a place, on such a day, I believe it. The lovely city hums with the excitement and anticipation of the opera. The rubbish lunch and forgettable pre-opera dinner are forgotten, we're in perfect position in the arena – Row 10. The old stadium is packed – thousands of people – and high up on each side candles, torches, cigarette lighters glitter as darkness falls, and we concentrate on the stage. It's enormous, with a great hand in the middle, reaching for the sky, part of a huge, uncompleted statue for the church in which the tragic drama is set. The staging is spectacular, magnificent setting, hundreds of extras, wonderfully mar-shalled by the great Zeffirelli himself. The singing is not too shabby either, and then the tenor lets fly with his big moment, the aria 'E lucevan le stelle' – the stars are brightly shining. This is my first time in Italy at an opera, and I'm not prepared for what happens next: he finishes, to a huge roar of applause, and when it has died down to a dull roar, he sings it again! An encore? In the middle of an opera? We didn't do it that way when I was a 'singer' at the Dublin Grand Opera in the Gaiety, all those years ago. We don't do it at Garsington or Glyndebourne, no matter how brilliant the soloist. It's not done. Except in Italy, the home of grand opera, where the art is a spontaneous, living entertainment, and if the boy or girl done good, let 'em do it again. And again. Nobody's rushing for a bus, and nobody here thinks that just because you get into a black tie, you have to behave like a stuffed dummy. What a blinding, unforgettable night.

We make our way home through the main square. It's heaving with beautiful young people, and although it's ringed with cafés and bars, chairs and tables, they're all standing around, chatting, laughing, flirting and drinking. There's no drunkenness, no loutish behaviour. Anything less like a British town on a Friday night would be hard to imagine.

26 August 2006

Madame Butterfly is again a triumph of stagecraft, teeming with extras and chorus, the Japanese houses and village realised to perfection, but, after the magnificence of *Tosca* and the excitement of the first night in the great arena, somehow, it's an anti-climax. And the lovely, girlish, tragic, betrayed Cho-Cho-San is being played by a fifteen-stone Italian soprano, who gurgles on her top notes.

29 August 2006

That Ofcom banning of the *Tom and Jerry* cartoon, because the cat was smoking a roll-up cigarette, continues to have repercussions:

> *I thought you would like an update on my latest project. In association with the Jarrow Institute of Smoking in Movies, a team is apparently working round the clock to eradicate all smoking scenes from every film ever made.*
>
> *Work is progressing well on the Humphrey Bogart back catalogue, with some films ending up so short they fit neatly onto a 25-minute podcast.* The Big Sleep *has become 'The Short Nap',* The Maltese Falcon *is now a sparrow, and* The African Queen *runs out of steam halfway through the first reel.*
>
> *We have had particular success with Jean-Luc Goddard's first film, the appropriately named* Breathless. *By removing every scene containing smoking, the entire film has been reduced to a shot of Jean Seberg walking down the Champs Elysées . . .*
>
> *Some film titles will have to be updated too. We've started with* Smokey and the Bandit, *which is now 'Friendly Bacteria and the Premium Rate Phone Quiz'.*
>
> DES CUSTARD OF TUNBRIDGE WELLS

Ever on the qui vive for new ideas and names, the *grands fromages* of TV drama are skipping about with glee at an entirely new concept that will star the rarely seen James Nesbitt, Amanda Burton, Ross Kemp, Tamsin Outhwaite and a raft of ex-*Corrie* and *'stenders* actors. High time the powers-that-be went out on a limb and took a risk with casting. The show will be set in a hospital A and E cum veterinary surgery cum medical practice cum police station, following the doings of James Nesbitt's character, Harry Cole.

Nesbitt plays an undercover doctor, vet, police inspector who also has a thriving legal practice. The working title is *Cole's Law* . . . That was from Rex Fittup, Friend to the Stars. As I've said, *ad nauseam*, I only read 'em.

9 September 2006

It's another musical evening – this time it's Proms in the Park or, if you like, Proms in the Dark, Prawns in the Park, or any other name by which you care to call this precious rose. I suppose I've been compèring it for the past ten years, but, as I've said before, these days I'm not much of a judge. The Park in question is Hyde, and there are 40,000 people out there who don't give a tinker's curse if the heavens open as they did last year – they're here to laugh and cheer, wave their flags, eat, drink and be merry, before seeing off the Last Night of the Proms with 'Jerusalem', 'Land of Hope and Glory' and the rest, at the top of their voices. As ever, Ken Bruce started the whole thing at 5.30 p.m., with a lively farrago of pop that roused the crowd to the requisite frenzy, before I took to the stage to introduce the BBC Concert Orchestra under Carl Davis.

Carl likes to dress up for these occasions, and it doesn't go unnoticed:

> *Tell me one thing . . . why was the conductor dressed as a*
> *chef? With a little red serviette in his top pocket?*
> *I half expected him to come back on with a platter con-*
> *taining the great British roast dinner. Or a buffet of finger*
> *food to keep the masses of revellers happy.*
> *Or did I get it wrong? Perhaps he was dressed as a dentist?*
> *The thing is: you don't know nowadays.*
>
> SARAH-FIONA

> *Is the conductor from last night's proms hard up because he*
> *was dressed as if he was selling ice creams in the interval.*
>
> HORATIO HORNBLOWER

I don't know – a man does his best, and what thanks does he get for it?

Proms this year was a humdinger: two of the world's greatest opera stars, the soprano Angela Georghiou and the tenor Roberto Alagna; the beautiful trumpeter Alison Balsom; another tenor, the fast-rising Vittorio Grigolo; and to put the little tin hat on proceedings, the legendary pop star Lionel Richie.

It went magnificently, probably the best Prawns I've ever introduced to the Park. It's quite a complicated production, timing of the essence, as we link up with other live concerts in Northern Ireland, Wales and Scotland. The most crucial link-up is at the very end, where we have to join the Last Night of the Proms, up the road at the Albert Hall, so that 'Jerusalem' and all the other magnificent anthems can be synchronised for the benefit of our huge audience. Except that, tonight, the audience didn't want to let Lionel Richie go. They wanted more, and they didn't understand why I couldn't let them have any, that otherwise we'd miss the climax that was nearing at the Albert Hall. So, an audience who had greeted me with cheers and flags started to boo. What could I do? Grin and bear it – here comes 'Jerusalem'. Thank heaven – they were about to rush the platform.

12 September 2006

In years to come, when the sociologists of the future seek to discover where and when it all began to go pear-shaped for Blighty, they may well dismiss the moment Albert Tatlock took off his cap in the Rovers Return, in favour of the advent of the present obsession of councils all over the land with recycling. A listener tells me that in Worcester the council kindly invited citizens to attend a meeting, where they could be introduced to, inspect and ask any pertinent questions about wheelie-bins. The listener passed up the God-given opportunity in favour of watching the paint dry on his new back door, but he did come across an eight-page leaflet explaining the difference between the green and the grey bin, detailing the arrangements necessary if one lived in a flat, indicating what to do if the bin becomes over-full (apparently, you re-sort the rubbish to see if anything can go in the *larger* recycling bin), instructing you to make sure that your bin is out before seven in the morning and warning you to care for your bin, lest you have to pay for a new one, telling you how to avoid a smelly bin by washing your rubbish first, and, most importantly, how to identify your bin, although you may not put any markings on it. The listener says that she is training her bins to come to heel when called . . .

Another long-suffering resident reports that the bin police recently returned (with much pursing of the lips and clicking of the teeth) a champagne cork that she had foolishly placed in the wrong bin.

Wheelie-bin training

13 September 2006

The final indication, at least for this week, of decline and fall, is the latest Health and Safety edict on bicycle bells. Put aside your blind panic over the wave of gun crime, street violence, mugging, rape and the evil that threatens to engulf us all, and pay attention to that bell on your bike, if you don't want the law to come down on you like a ton of bricks. Only today a South Devon listener described how she pedals through the narrow streets, belting along at ten miles per hour without her bell, and no means of warning the forty-foot-long pantechnicons, the cars, caravans and tractors as they overtake her with at least two inches to spare. She said that she could be the first person in the country to be posthumously awarded the No Bell Peace Prize, for cycling quietly.

I am reminded of an old Dublin saying: 'There I was, with no bell on me bike – but me knickers wringing . . .'

14 September 2006

A free leaflet delivered to Hertfordshire residents (more stuff for the recycling bin) says that speeding drivers in the county may be offered the opportunity to attend a national speed awareness course, instead of picking up the usual fixed-penalty fine. The courses will last for six hours and include both a classroom and a practical session, at a cost of £100. But, doesn't a fixed-penalty speeding offence incur a fine of only £60? It's a fair cop, officer, take me away . . .

They're sensitive in Hertfordshire: a listener there accused one of my hand-picked band of underlings (aka 'newsreaders') of mispronouncing the proud county as 'Harfordshire', but it was only an excuse to recount the classic tale of another missing 'T'. On the occasion when the Hollywood blonde bombshell of the Thirties, Jean Harlow, met the frosty British lady and MP Margot Asquith, Miss Harlow greeted her with 'Oh! you must be Margot Asquith!' 'No, dear, it's Marg*ot*. The "T" is silent, as in Harlow . . .' 'Tongue like an adder,' as the great Cliff Morgan once said to me of a female acquaintance.

The word 'celebrity' should be taken out and shot, since it has no meaning any more. It is, however, the linchpin, the vital cog that makes the media go round. Do you remember when we used to criticise all the makeover, gardening, interior decorating and holiday programmes that cluttered up our television screens, every hour on the hour? We didn't know we were born! Look at us now, quailing under the weight of 'celebrity' television: *I'm a Celebrity, Get Me Out of Here, X-Factor, Celebrity Strictly Come Dancing, Celebrity Fat Club, Celebrity Stars In Their Eyes, Celebrity Love Island, The Two of Us* (otherwise known to sufferers as 'Celebrity Come Singing').

Even as I write we've got something my TOGs call 'Celebrity Stuff It Down Your Gob'. It's not the efforts with pan and skillet of the celebs, bless 'em, which catch the eye, however. It's the almost obscene manner in which the two judges fork the food into their mouths. They open their capacious maws like traps, and shovel the stuff in. One of them is a chef, fair enoughski, but the other judge was described in the first series as a 'greengrocer'. Lo, and behold, this time he's an 'ingredients expert'. 'How do you become an ingredients expert?' a listener wants to know. 'Do you study the packaging of foods and commit all the ingredients to memory, then sit a test to prove you know what's in a box of cornflakes or a frozen lasagne?'

On the other hand, what's an 'artist'? Or, for that matter, what's 'art'? Anything, apparently, the artist wants to call art. A bit like 'celebrity' . . .

The celebrity chef has become a phenomenon, an artist in his own right. The art of cooking – the only art that disappears almost as soon as it's produced. Like everything, it can go too far. In a Tesco today, one of my spies saw Donuts [*sic*] *designed* by Marco Pierre White. A round lump of fried dough – how do you design that, Marco P?

It's one of the beauties of email that I get an instant reaction every time I open my mouth. Mention of the Donut provoked several observers to remember a year or so ago, when Ainsley Harriott's name and face were on packs of sausages. The cooking advice was 'prick with a fork'. They flew off the shelves . . .

Puts me in mind of the apocryphal tale told of the turkey king, Bernard Matthews. He did his own television commercials, until the day he stood in front of the camera, smiled and intoned: 'Try my turkeys. They're Norfolk, and good.' Say it quickly to yourself . . .

16 September 2006

These are testing times for ITV with advertising revenue sliding and the chief executive getting the bum's rush, but even a casual inspection of that channel's afternoon viewing might well give a clue to what's amiss. It's a relentless barrage of ambulance-chasing lawyers, funeral expenses, dogs and elephants selling insurance, loans that will beggar your family for generations to come, stairlifts, walk-in baths, remedies for incontinence, diarrhoea, constipation, ladies' leakage, friendly bacteria and varnish that does what it says on the tin. You don't think that ITV's decline might be due to factors other than its programmes?

And while I'm at it, just how many episodes of *Murder, She Wrote* did Angela Lansbury make? She's on twice a day, week in, week out. And *Columbo*. Oh God, don't tell me in twenty years' time we'll be watching endless repeats of *EastEnders*.

20 September 2006

With customary *élan*, the BBC is producing a weekly podcast of *Wake Up To Wogan*, a fifteen-minute farrago of the best bits, without any music, because that's illegal. I didn't ask . . . Mercifully it'll do little damage, because, as ever, the old Corporation imagines that the public will get to know about this breakthrough by a process of osmosis and without any publicity whatsoever. It's something that dear Biddy Beeb has never been very good at, blowing its own trumpet. The Radio 2 website is a case in point, updated so infrequently that they still thought I was on holiday, two weeks after my return. The *Children in Need* website is nothing more than a 'couldn't care less' disgrace. No wonder some of my listeners think that our new slogan is, 'Radio 2 – where indifference works'.

As soon as my listeners heard about the podcast, skin and hair flew in all directions. An Och Aye Pod for Scotland, a Dai Pod for the Welsh and a Why Aye Pod for the North-East. Then a plod-cast for the police, a lie pod for politicians, a diddley-eye-dye pod for the Irish, for high-flying lovers, the mile-high pod, and for tourists, the London-Eye pod.

As for most of my listeners, it's all a mystery to me. I'm going to have to wait a couple of years until my eldest grandson is four and can show me how to do it.

22 September 2006

All is excitement – at least among those who care – about the Ryder Cup, the biennial golf match which features Great Britain and Europe versus the United States. Despite the fact that the Americans consider their golf tour and their golfers superior to ours, the last few encounters have gone resoundingly Great Britain and Europe's way. Match- and team-play are foreign to American golf pros; their game is a solitary, every-man-for-himself pursuit. So hopes are high for this year's confrontation, particularly as it's being played on the K-Club course, just outside Dublin. I know from my Irish friends that Dublin, and indeed Ireland, has been subsumed by the contest, so, having heard the weather forecast, I speculated what it was doing across the Irish Sea. Rain is not unknown there – wasn't I myself born and married in a downpour – so it was unsurprising but nonetheless upsetting to get the latest from an Irish listener: 'Well, to give you some idea – we sowed an acre of lawn on Saturday and it now resembles the Atlantic Ocean. There's a flock of seagulls circling, as I write.'

Further reports that they were painting the grass of the K-Club green so as not to disappoint American viewers of the Emerald Isle, I discounted publicly, but privately believed. A listener tells me that they went to the practice day today and couldn't understand why people coming from the opposite direction on the public walkways kept bumping into him. The signs he was reading at 100-metre intervals clearly stated: 'Pedestrians Walk to the Right.' It was only when he looked at the other side of them that he realised the problem. On the other side he read: 'Pedestrians Walk to the Left.'

24 September 2006

So the lads won, amid scenes of great emotion and pints of the black stuff. Darren Clarke was the Irish hero, having risen above personal tragedy, and the United States team took their thrashing in sportsmanlike fashion. But then, they're used to it. The grandiose opening extravaganza had featured a glamorous blonde in a ballgown despite the fact that it was the afternoon, and the closing ceremony was kicked off by a group of musicians dressed as though they'd just finished repairing the road. A great and glorious victory, and, if I know anything, it'll take Dublin a week to recover. The Crooked Man of Old Bangor Town, as always, had a stave or two in praise of the day:

> *What a wonderful sight was Darren's delight*
> *When the Ryder Cup was won.*
> *Such K-Club joys for Woosie's boys;*
> *Even Casey got a hole in one.*
>
> *I bet they got squiffy down by the Liffey*
> *When the Tiger's roar was dimmed.*
> *And the testimonials of those ex-colonials*
> *By our Euro-lads were trimmed.*
>
> *The gallery's cheers which moved Darren to tears*
> *Were sportsmanship shining bright.*
> *Now the whole Emerald Isle is one big smile*
> *As it shares in Darren's delight.*

25 September 2006

Some days are diamonds, some days are stones, as the good ol' country song has it. There are other fine country ballads such as 'How can I miss you, if you won't go away?', but they need not detain us here. Some days, the 600-odd, and very odd, emails that Barrowlands Boyd, aka Beryl Ann Boyd, aka Hopalong, prints off and dumps on my lap every morning glitter like gemstones; other days, it's the needle in the haystack. There's no pattern, no rhyme nor reason. Today, I threw out emails that I would gladly have used on a less inspirational day. I hold very few letters overnight – I like to think that the listener and I can take our chances together every morning, and damn the torpedoes. I don't know where that last phrase came from, probably some black-and-white Second World War epic, but it has stuck in my mind, and now my listeners expect it of me in moments of high drama, usually just before I crash into the eight o'clock pips. Just as they expect 'You'll never miss your mother 'til she's buried 'neath the clay' when someone writes from a far-flung corner of the old Empire, saying how much they miss my homespun philosophising. Or 'set a spell, and let your saddle cool' after some yodelling from an eejit in a Stetson. But here, I've gone walkabout . . .

It was hundreds of little things this morning, well, thousands of them. The country's sinking under a plague of crane-flies – daddy-long-legs, harmless little creatures with a disconcerting habit of detaching a limb if you even look at them. Naturally, my listener takes a sideways view:

They're absolutely everywhere. Great long spindly things, in your face, no useful purpose in life. Apparently the weather conditions have been ideal for them and have helped bring about this enormous glut. A blooming nuisance, if you ask me. Yes, you can't move for gladioli.

The supermarkets are practically giving them away. Personally, I blame Dame Edna.

DES CUSTARD OF TUNBRIDGE WELLS

Then there was a news item (slow news day) about the prospect of genetically engineered hypo-allergenic cats. Many thought that an allergy to cats might well be nature's way of saying 'no cats for you'. Maybe the boffins could more profitably engineer a moggy that didn't rip up your bin bags in the night.

Someone wrote in to tell me one of the listed hazards in the job specification of a Community Safety Officer for Hampshire County Council: 'Exposure to Non Ionising Radiation'. That'll be the sun, then . . .

I think I can claim the credit for introducing the American euphemism for the forgetfulness of old age, 'a senior moment', to Britain. Which is why I and my fellow TOGs were scandalised to hear from Bob, an NHS employee in Bury, Lancs, that he and his colleagues were recently instructed by their Personnel (sorry, Human Resources) Department that the elderly can no longer be described as having a

Don't say it

'senior moment'. Apparently, it's in breach of the new age discrimination legislation. I think I'm going to have to lie down now . . .

26 September 2006

Who'd be a Prime Minister? What insane force could drive anyone to spend their lives in the very eye of the tornado, sure in the knowledge that all that lies at the end of the storm is abuse, ingratitude and scorn? For that has been the lot of every British Prime Minister in my lifetime going back even to the great war lord, Winston Churchill. And it's got worse in the last couple of decades: Thatcher, Major and now Tony Blair. And, apart from the Royal Family, no other family in the land is more in the glare of the limelight and the flash of the paparazzi than that of the Prime Minister. From the beginning, the British press have had it in for Cherie Blair and yesterday they tried to hang her out to dry again, as a passing journalist reported her comment, as she watched Gordon Brown speaking: 'That's a lie!' My listeners, ever ready to misinterpret, mislead and deliberately mishear, felt that as the comment was made as Cherie was leaving, it could just as easily have been 'Cheery-bye!', or even 'What a guy!' Of course! That's what it was! They just don't want to print the good news, do they?

27 September 2006

At long last, the BBC has given the old heave-ho to these station identification snippets with dancers in the rain, tai-chi in the hills, tap dancers, kick-boxers, skateboarders and the rest, which were so reflective of life in Britain today. The theme of the new ones appears to be along the lines of life as a circle. There are footballers, kite-flyers, surfers and, most intriguing of all, hippopotamuses. It all signifies the new BBC watchword of 'diversity'. Someone pointed out that while we're all increasingly aware that global warming is a clear and ever-present danger and within minutes Bridlington will be as warm as Benidorm, we wouldn't expect hippos to be wading ashore at Folkestone for a few years yet. A less charitable contributor asked tartly if the BBC could not have saved the millions this nonsense, and particularly the hippos, cost, and just filmed Chris Moyles and me having a swim at the local pool.

To the old Haunted Doughnut, the BBC TV Centre, for a chat with Paul O'Grady, who records his daily Channel 4 show there. I never really liked Paul as Lily Savage, precisely because he was too savage, too tart for me, as that character. What a stroke of genius to give him his own talk show, as himself. Who could have thought that he would turn out to be the most relaxed, charming, witty, chat-show host on the box. His success has been instant, and deserved. So, it's always a pleasure to appear on his show, like chatting to a friend – an easy, generous friend. I was there to whip book-buyers into a maelstrom of delight at the prospect of buying my new oeuvre, *Mustn't Grumble*, just about to hit the bookshelves of Britain. That's why people do talk shows, you know, to promote their book, their film, their television programme. They don't do them to reveal hitherto unknown facts about themselves, their vices or their peccadilloes. Everybody knows this, including critics, who still from time to time feel it necessary to have a go at chat-show hosts for being bland and sycophantic. Paxman does the probing, incisive question thing, but that's the political arena, and they expect it. The public have voted for them, they've got to answer. Any light entertainment chat-show host trying dear Jeremy's scornful routine on their guests would find themselves without a soul to sit on their seats or settee within a week.

The *Paul O'Grady Show* signals the beginning of the pilgrimage that all authors must endure – the book-signing tour. I'm off to Dublin in a couple of days, then Birmingham, Windsor, Kirkham, Milton Keynes and the rest. I'll be telling you the gory details as we go.

29 September 2006

Off to Dublin in the green! As soon as I finish my Radio 2 show, I'm into another studio to do an interview with Gerry Ryan, a good friend and a blinding broadcaster, who does a morning show in Ireland on RTE that would leave most British broadcasters in the shade. The RTE I left behind in 1970 was a pale imitation of the BBC Home Service. After the birth of the Irish Free State, Ireland's broadcasting service had been set up along the lines of the Mother, the Auntie, of all broadcasters and little had changed in the intervening forty years. Now, when I listen to Irish radio, it's a blast of fresh air, probably the most outspoken and free-thinking in Europe. Much of that is due to Gerry Ryan, who broke the mould – nothing is taboo. British phone-in hosts who think they're dicing with danger are only in the ha'penny place, as the Granny used to say. In rural Ireland, the radio is local to the nth degree. Their most popular programmes are the death notices. Marriages and births come a poor second.

Flying across with the brothers' airline, Aer Lingus, I am reminded of the Irish stewardess who asks the passenger if he'd like lunch. 'What's on the menu?' 'Well, there's chicken, beef, salmon or duck.' 'Oh, what's the duck like?' 'It's like a chicken, but it swims.' In the hungry Fifties and Sixties, to be an Aer Lingus hostess was the ultimate for every well-brought-up, convent-educated girl in Ireland. Superior girls, who poured you a drink and delivered your food as if they were doing you a favour: 'There you go.'

Tonight is the reunion of the Class of '56, Belvedere College. Fifty years on, thirty-two of us gather in the old school for Mass, then drinks and dinner in the splendid Georgian dining room of the old house where the Jesuits, our teachers, lived. No more; the teachers are lay men and women. One of Ireland's great schools, if not its greatest, its academic and sporting traditions are more than sustained. The facilities, the courses on offer leave us shaking our heads; the former Captain of School says to me, 'You know, you and I wouldn't be good enough to get into this school today.'

Here we are, fifty years older, and nobody's changed. On the outside, perhaps, but the characters are the same as I left them, all those years ago. Of course, we are changed by circumstances, by the accidents of life, but most of these fellows came from comfortable, successful, middle-class backgrounds, and they have maintained the even tenor of their lives. They've never left the district of Dublin they were born in, never mind Ireland. Good-humoured, warm-hearted, the best of the Emerald Isle.

30 September 2006

It's chucking it down, which is no surprise, as Mick Devine's son drives me to Easons bookstore, Dawson Street, Dublin. Although the Irish are well used to 'soft' conditions, I don't expect huge numbers of people to queue up in the driving rain for the doubtful privilege of having the likes of me scrawl across a book. Still, there's a jolly crowd, many of them British tourists, and a couple who've travelled all the way from Northern Ireland. Then, two youngish men are standing before me. 'We're Chuffer Dandridge,' they say in unison. I can't believe it! Chuffer Dandridge, who writes to me every day, an old Shakespearian actor-manager, permanently resting, and, like Mr Pickwick, ever-expectant that something will turn up, such as the white fiver he lent Larry when they were both in rep. These two apparently normal, sane people, are both Irish civil servants – where do they get all that Sindenesque luvvie dialogue?

I'm still thinking about it as I land in Heathrow, and head straight for my son Alan's birthday party. It's tomorrow really, but he's combining his big day with an even bigger one – Alan's just become engaged to the lovely, warm and bright Kate Slade. Both our other children, Mark and Katherine, married three years ago. Can't wait for Alan and Kate's big day on

9 December. The organising is being done by Mike and Heather Slade, which is a relief, since Helen and I did our stuff for both Katherine and Mark in 2003. Actually, I suspect Helen would love to be more involved, but I got away scot-free in the wedding-speech stakes. I can eat and drink without a care. Though strangely enough, one way or another, I always end up on my feet.

Hurrah! According to the latest government-funded research, we have the best motorway system in the world, although this information will come as a rude awakening to those moaning minnies who never stop whingeing on, just because they spend most of their lives sitting in stationary vehicles on the M5, 25, 4, 40, 6, 52, etc., etc. The above kind of assertion, flying as it does in the face of all received knowledge, follows in the fine tradition of the announcement a couple of years ago that 'traffic-calming' measures were being put in place on motorways, because the slower you go, the quicker you get there. The logical conclusion to this being that, if you stop altogether, you'll be there even quicker. Any moment now, someone will tell us that the pound in our pockets will be unaffected by tax increases, interest rates or global warming. It's been a rainy month, but no possibility of drought conditions being lifted – it's the wrong kind of rain. I can see it: falling at a slant, bouncing off the ground.

2 October 2006

To Borders bookshop, Birmingham. It's like the Hampton Court maze. Underpasses, overpasses – how does anyone find their way around this planning disaster of a city? Shouldn't have wasted my time anyway – about forty people turned up, all of them because they heard me plug it on the radio this morning. Still, it's worth doing to meet the TOGs. They quietly pass over their books, ask me to sign, and then tell me who they really are. Well, actually, they tell me who they're not – they give me the pseudonyms under which they write to the radio show. Maybe the false names are the real them, or the people they want to be. Perhaps I should write a monograph on the psychological significance of this insight. If I ever get out of Birmingham . . .

3 October 2006

That's better – Ottakar's Bookshop, Windsor. Properly organised public appearance – efficient staff, good display, big crowd – must have signed a couple of hundred books. Book-signing is different from what it was six years ago for my first autobiography, *Is It Me?* Now, everybody has a mobile phone with a camera, so everything takes twice as long – sign book, pose for picture. Last time, I got repetitive strain injury from all the signing; this time I'm sure it'll be lockjaw as well, from all the smiling. Interesting that BBC Books have re-issued *Is It Me?* A rising tide lifts all boats . . .

4 October 2006

Lewis Carnie of Radio 2 and that smart queen of promotion, Jackie Gill, came up with the bright idea of selling the seats for an opening preview of *Wicked*, a Broadway smash-hit musical about to open in the West End, for *Children in Need*. Tonight's the night, and I'm making the introductions from the stage of the Victoria Palace. Into the old black tie – why can't I tie the bloody thing, after all these years? Helen, as ever, does the needful. In through the stage door, up the back stairs, the cast and chorus milling around in fantastic costumes appropriate to a musical about the Witches of Oz, before Dorothy set off with Toto down the yellow-brick road. Peek through the curtains; the theatre is full to bursting. Good for the children! On I go.

It's a great show – good music, good singing, sparkling per-formances, spectacular staging. Afterwards, it's off to the Goring Hotel for a reception with the cast, celebrities (a dying breed) and those who have paid through the nose to help *Children in Need*. Those remarkable TOGs, Hellen Bach and Norm, tell me that, with unpaid and unsung help from fellow TOGs, they're posting out *Janet and John* CDs, not by the hundred, but by the thousand. It's certainly the best-selling CD in the country, but all sales are via the Internet or post, so are not recorded in record shops. Despite kindly old Gordo taking his whack of VAT – a thundering disgrace on a charit-able, unpaid, non-profit-making enterprise – they tell me the amount raised for *Children in Need* so far is close to £800,000. I know I'm a cock-eyed optimist, but I think it's going to reach the million-pound mark by the big night, 17 November. What an evening!

5 October 2006

So, what's the first email that catches my eye this morning?

Last night, we were at the Apollo Victoria for a night with the stars. At last the moment arrived and out you came on to the stage to rapturous applause. The cheers, the excitement as we waited for the pearls of wisdom that would fall from your lips. Then the man next to me leaned across and whispered, 'Who is he?'

Turned out he was Norwegian – thank goodness he wasn't Danish – you were only 10 rows in front of us and I might not have been able to restrain him!

Show was brilliant though – thanks to everyone involved.

VIV PARSONS

8 October 2006

Helen's off to France with a group of like-minded ladies whom she calls 'the girls'. They'll play golf and bridge and never stop talking. And as soon as they get home from holiday, they'll phone each other up for an hour-long chat. I'll never get through half the stuff she's pre-cooked and left in the freezer for me. They'll stay in Château de Polignac, a lovely house that we bought ten years ago in the south-west of France. It's in a tree-filled park, surrounded by vines, in the middle of tranquil countryside, an area famous for d'Artagnan, Armagnac and duck. If you don't like duck in our part of La Belle, you're dead. The château is really a *maison de maître*, and the biggest house in a hamlet of four others, so they call it a château. We love it for its peace and pure air – and the drink and ducks, of course.

I won't have a lot of time to miss Helen – next week it's book-signing. Mind you, I'm joining Helen in France on Friday, anyway . . .

9 October 2006

As soon as the radio show comes to a grinding halt, I'm off like a redshank, as the Granny used to say, to Battersea heliport, and up, up and away in the general direction of Blackpool. Not the gem in the diadem of Britain's seaside resorts itself, but a little town named Kirkham, and a bookshop called Silverdell. With the Tower in the distance, and beyond it the grey Irish Sea, we land in a farmer's field, kindly lent by a friend of Silverdell's owners.

They lay out a red carpet from the helicopter to the gate, and the welcome is warm. The whole day is bathed in a warm glow. Kirkham's in the middle of nowhere, but the crowd is huge, and everybody seems to know everybody else. I don't care if they've come to see me, or buy a home-made ice cream, which is what Silverdell sells, along with books. The two ladies who started it began trading as an ice-cream café, and the books business crept up on them while their backs were turned. It's one of the most successful independent booksellers in the country – and the Baileys Irish ice cream is none too shabby, either.

After a couple of glorious flights, during which we enjoyed seeing England in its sun-kissed best, as the helicopter approaches the Thames Valley I could see the storm clouds festering. We land at White Waltham airfield just as the heavens open. I swim home. Timing, it's a gift . . .

10 October 2006

The Heights is a restaurant at the top of St George's Hotel, just around the corner from Broadcasting House, which offers a splendid view of London, and over the years it has become a sort of broadcasters' annexe. It's where I hold most of my meetings, such as they are, and this morning it is the turn of Elaine Paterson, producer of *Children in Need*. Elaine is nothing short of brilliant. She has produced this behemoth of live television programmes for the past five years, without ever losing her cool, her temper, her charm or her extraordinary ability to put together seven hours of live entertainment that regularly gain one of the year's biggest television audiences and in 2005 raised a record-breaking £17 million in one night. She's as cool and even-tempered as ever, but the pressure is enormous to produce an even bigger and better fundraiser this year. Elaine has a great team, and in Nick Vaughan-Barrett an executive producer of tremendous ability and experience, who has been responsible for the television coverage of every great British occasion of the last ten years. As always, though, at this time, with about four weeks to go, everything's up in the air. Stars are in, out, in again, there's a list of 'maybes' as long as your arm. *Coronation Street*, who were brilliant last year, can't do it.

EastEnders have no time. We're going to do a special *Deal or No Deal* with Noel Tidybeard, and then suddenly we're not. We had Madonna open the show last year; this year it looks like I'll have to break into song. Don't panic, Mr Mainwaring!

My friend Richard Ingrams has asked me to address an *Oldie* literary lunch at Simpsons on the Strand. I usually do my bit for the *Oldie* at their award-giving ceremony at the same venue in March, but this time I've got to get up and extol the virtues of *Mustn't Grumble.* The audience is on your side, otherwise they wouldn't spend good money on a lunch for your benefit, so literary lunches are usually fun, and people rarely throw the cutlery. I particularly remember last time round, at a *Daily Mail* lunch, sharing the stand with the late Linda Lee-Potter. She stole the show by never referring to her book and giving a knockabout performance on the great and the good she had interviewed, and sometimes decapitated. She understood that people had come to see and hear her, their favourite columnist. The book they could buy and read later.

12 October 2006

Ottakar's of Milton Keynes, land of the concrete cow, yesterday. The place is a series of roundabouts, surrounded by car parks. Obviously, it's Britain's answer to Los Angeles. Nobody walks anywhere. Today it's 'Gatport Airwick', as my old chum Ray Moore was given to say. Toulouse, here I come . . .

16 October 2006

Me again. Who says I take too-long holidays? Refreshed and revived by bounteous Gers, I'm ready for the week. I'll be banjaxed at the end of it: Tuesday, Guildford; Wednesday, Nottingham; Friday, Glasgow; Saturday, Edinburgh. We're all doomed, anyway. In order to keep us in line, the powers that be trot out a scare a week. This week, it's obesity. We're the fat boy of Europe, the Brits have eaten all the pies, and unless we straighten up and fly right, we're for the knackers. It's hell up North – they can expect the Grim Reaper a good two years before Southern softies. One Northern listener of mine has devolved a cunning plan: when he's at death's door, he will, with all speed, move south of the Watford Gap, thus cheating Old Father Time out of an extra two years. But didn't 'research show' that we're all living longer? And we're going to have to work until we're called to our eternal reward, as well, now that

Obesity epidemic

pensions are a dead duck. Another gnarled listener thinks that the main role of old people nowadays is to make profits for nursing homes. He claims to have come up with the ideal solution. Why not build big houses where old people can work? We could call them 'workhouses'.

18 October 2006

Yesterday, Guildford. Today I find myself at WH Smith Nottingham, another masterpiece of town planning. Question: if you're building a motorway, wouldn't you try to build it as close to your main cities as possible? It's a ten-mile drive, at least, along a narrow country road, from the motorway to Nottingham, and Leicester is miles away from its motorway link as well. Anyway, here I am at last behind a desk groaning under the weight of copies of *Mustn't Grumble*. Behind me are posters featuring the book, my name and photos of our hero. In front of the desk are two large placards bearing my name and likeness. As I sign the fly-leaf for an eager purchaser, I hear a passing customer enquire of an assistant: 'Who is it?'

I get a letter from a listener whose doctor's surgery has recently updated its technology. Having had his annual blood tests, he was told to ring for the results the following week between eleven and twelve noon. As he was passing the surgery at that time, he popped in and asked for the results. The receptionist was strict, but fair: 'Sorry but you must phone between eleven and twelve noon for test results.' 'But I was passing, so I'm here.' 'Sorry, you must phone in.' My correspondent backed off a couple of paces, and phoned the surgery on his mobile. The receptionist answered, and quickly gave him the results he wanted. It's life, Jim, but not as we know it . . .

Please call

19 October 2006

The Archers, which used to be 'an everyday story of country folk' has turned before our very ears into a steamy tale of illicit sex behind the cowsheds. It's not easy to take for the delicately reared and those used to more bucolic excitements, such as liver-fluke and staggers among the sheep. 'I stopped listening to *The Archers* just after Grace was killed in the fire and about the time that Phil had a heated discussion with Dan about which breed of pig to buy. As I recall, there was something about Saddlebacks, Large Whites and the best return for the money. Then they all got swine-fever or something. All of limited interest to a lad from Lewisham. I never really forgave *The Archers* for replacing *Dick Barton, Special Agent.*'(Rebecca of Sunnybrook Farm.) Me neither; I cried. Still smarting after all these years.

And then some smart alec wrote to say that Dick Barton was replaced not by *The Archers*, but by something called *The Dangerous Dexters*, an everyday story of circus folk. It didn't last long. The lead character fell off the trapeze and broke his neck . . . allegedly.

21 October 2006

I'm in Edinburgh, in the Gyle Centre. Huge crowd, everything taking twice as long because, as usual, everybody wants a photo on their mobile phone as well as an autograph in *Mustn't Grumble*. What is this strange power I have over the Scots? Yesterday, at Argyle Street in Glasgow, another endless queue, and the ultimate compliment: I got a bigger crowd than the last book-signing by a Glasgow Rangers/Celtic football star.

The queues for the book-signings have been bigger than for *Is It Me?* six years ago. That went to number one for weeks on the bestsellers list, but the best I've done this time so far is number five. Looking back, I see that I was at number one with sales of 5,000 per week. This time, I'm selling five times that number, and I'm only in the middle of the Top Ten. In six short years, the whole book-buying game has changed; now it's the Internet and the supermarkets that dictate who's top of the pile. There's a whole new market for books out there. Folk who've never bought a book in their lives are buying biographies of Sharon Osbourne, Jordan and people who are famous for making eejits of themselves in the Big Brother House. I blame Richard and Judy . . .

26 October 2006

As the Old Geezers gear themselves up for the annual assault on their nerves that is Halloween, a neighbourhood group I know are going to give Guy Fawkes a break this year. Instead, they're going to set ablaze an effigy of someone, who they claim has caused more pain, suffering, misery and damage to the good of the nation than a thousand Gunpowder Plots. Yes, they're going to set fire to a Health and Safety officer. They were going to burn a Health and Safety Rule Book as well, but feared the resultant conflagration would beggar the Great Fire of London.

God knows, I'm not a risk-taker – how people can ski, bungee-jump, fling themselves out of aeroplanes, clamber up precipices or down holes in the ground is beyond me. However, in common with most people who are on the whole sane, I recognise that life is a risky business and that every time you walk out of your front door you're taking a chance. You're taking an even bigger chance if you stay indoors, because that's where most accidents occur. The nation cannot be wrapped in cotton wool – the government has got to stop thinking like Holden Caulfield in *The Catcher in the Rye*. We can't all be saved from falling over, yet the other day a gentleman friend who installs automatic swimming pool covers at £8,000 a throw was told by a client the reason why he had to have a safety pool cover that you could walk on. The client lived in a wealthy but high-crime area, and if ever an intruder were spotted in his garden, for health and safety reasons the local police would not be able to engage in hot pursuit unless such a cover was fitted.

And, of course, firemen are not allowed to slide down their poles any more. As Jim Davison used to say, as a joke: 'Too risky.'

30 October 2006

Sir Nicholas Stern, a former chief economist at the World Bank, has just issued a 700-word report, commissioned by good ol' Golden Brown, which forecasts floods, famine, mass movement of people and the destruction of species if the Earth's temperature continues to rise. Sir Nicholas is not a scientist or a meteorologist; he's not even a zoologist, like the government's chief adviser on climate change. The man's an economist. He's no fool, though. When, in twenty years' time, we've all been taxed to hell and back in the name of the environment, and Sweet Fanny Adams has happened to justify this apocalyptic vision, he'll claim the credit for saving us from Armageddon. The best way to cut carbon emissions would be for us all to breathe less frequently, and for maximum effect give up breathing altogether. Although this would tend to leave the government's plan to get us all fitter in a bit of a quandary.

Another plan, since plants and trees emit carbon dioxide in the dark, would be to leave the lights on all over Britain all night. Which, in turn, might well defeat the government's objective to conserve power and energy. Not that any of it would make a blind bit of difference to man-made climate change while China and India go their merry way polluting right, left and centre. No chance, I suppose, of the good Sir Nicholas bending Beijing's ear? I think I can hear the laughter in Tiananmen Square from here . . .

It's reported that when Tony Blair got the 70,000 words from Sir Nicholas he said that it was the most important document he has received in all his time at Number 10 Downing Street. More important, then, than the one that said Saddam Hussein could destroy us in forty-five minutes, using nuclear weapons?

Stern is the modern-day equivalent of those poor old geezers who used to walk the streets with sandwich boards proclaiming 'The End of the World is Nigh'. The problem is that, while nobody took any notice of those deluded doom-mongers, people pay attention to Sir Nicholas. Well, when I say people, I mean politicians. Not the same thing. Arnie Schwarzenegger looks like saving his arse in California by jumping on the green bandwagon, David Cameron's been bleating on about it for months and now Tone and Gordy have hitched a ride on the climate change gravy-train, in fear that Dave has stolen a march on them. Cars, aeroplanes – the watchword is green taxes. Even when oil prices drop, keep the price of petrol high, otherwise those dastardly car owners will pollute even more. You've got to give it to them for cunning: create a climate of fear, and people will do anything to be safe.

This morning I heard some eejit talk of the disastrous consequences if London was flooded. And what are the chances of volcanoes in Manchester and earthquakes in Birmingham, if we don't increase taxes? And if the increased tax burden is still insufficient, what are the chances of the Earth being eaten by a huge goat?

31 October 2006

Halloween, and the TOGs are out in curmudgeonly force, up in arms against the young geezers who will make their lives a misery this very evening with incessant ringing on doorbells, and menacing cries of 'Trick or Treat!' This is an American import – whatever happened to 'Penny for the Guy!'? – although the implied threat is the same: hand over the money and/or the goodies, or your door gets kicked in. Well, it's not quite as bad as that, but close enough to it for the police to announce that they will be coming down like a ton of bricks on any youthful high spirits that turn into plain old hooliganism. And if you think that means any young troublemaker is going to get a clip round the ear from the boys in blue, you haven't been paying attention for the past few years. 'Now, then, sonny, on your way,' will be the height of it. George Dixon will be doing handsprings in his grave – although as I recall, he moved pretty slowly in life. We never forgave Dirk Bogarde for shooting the harmless old bobby in *The Blue Lamp*. 'Hand it over, son,' said George – and Bogarde shot 'im . . . He was subsequently resuscitated for television's *Dixon of Dock Green*. Nobody ever took a pot-shot at him again, although the great line, 'Watch out, Andy, he's got a shooter!' is for ever etched in my memory.

I see that I've come a long way from Halloween, but my TOGs were splenetic about it on the radio this morning, with plans to offer the little darlings chocolate-covered Brussels sprouts and toffee onions. Others were even more confrontational. 'I've got the bear traps in place, the spikes are smeared with poison, and my patented tar and feather machine is cunningly hidden behind the bushes of my garden path. Let 'em all come!' Bless . . .

I have tried numerous counter-measures.

1. *The old 'Lights out we are not at home', which resulted in the wee darlings shouting through the letter box, 'We know you are in there!!!'*

2. *The line 'We do not believe in Halloween' which was shot down by one of the accompanying parents saying, 'My mother remembers you coming round to our house when you were a lad.'*

3. *Last year's sign above the door reading 'Caution door bell gives electric shocks!!!', which just seemed to attract the children to dare each other to touch the bell, which meant it was ringing more than ever.*

So this year I have the solution that is sure to be a winner.

*As we all know, children these days are allergic to everything. So I plan to put a new sign above the door reading 'Caution! **This house may contain NUTS!!!'***

AL E CAT

Old doom-monger Stern's report continues to reverberate as it was designed to do: if ever there was a political scare-tactic to keep the voters on the straight and narrow . . . We're all doomed, but the bulldog spirit lives on.

Dear Leader,

I live on the sea front at Fleetwood, and although I can tell the nation this morning that the Irish Sea is, currently, on its own side of the sea wall, I'm taking no chances. The house is surrounded by a four-foot barrage of sand bags. All the furniture is upstairs, and the cars are up on four-foot ramps.

Fear not, we'll be OK. It's judgement that counts.

ANDY DEXTROUS

PS Isn't Stern an economist? . . . Could we have the future economic forecast done by a climatologist? You never know what you'll find do you?

The Americans have put the kibosh on Internet online gambling, but Tessa Jowell thinks this will force gambling underground, so why don't we tax it instead? It's the answer to everything: global warming, congestion, indigestion, ageing, overcrowding – you name it. Mind you, they're only doing it to benefit mankind . .

1 November 2006

It's another grandson! At ten to five this evening, Mark's wife, Susan, gave birth to a son, a seven-pounds-fourteen-ounces chap, and his name is Harry. It's our second grandchild, and about time . . . It's all been badly planned, and I blame my children. They all got married in their thirties – and Alan isn't even married yet (he will be in a month) – and Helen and I, well stricken in years, have the prospect of three or four little lunatics under the age of five, wrecking the place. Helen often says that she thought she was on the shelf, unmarried at twenty-five. I was pretty young, for an Irishman, to be married at twenty-six, but we'd have both thought ourselves in the last stages of decrepitude if we'd left it until our thirties.

He's a beautiful little boy, with his mother's lovely eyes and his father's muscles. The following morning I played the song 'Harry' on my morning show, and reduced Mark, Susan, and the rest of the family to tears, including myself . . .

2 November 2006

In late October 2006, the man who had been my radio producer for ten years, and a very dear friend for much longer than that, passed quietly to what I hope will be his eternal reward for a life well, honestly, decently and lovingly spent. I'll miss him, the BBC will miss him, the music business, his friends, his family, anybody whose life he ever touched will miss this lovely man. His name was Paul Christopher Walters, but the world knew him as 'Pauly'. Today, in his parish church of Kimpton, Hertfordshire, we held a service of celebration for his life and work. Canon Roger Royle, a friend and colleague, conducted it along with the vicar, Revd Lorraine Summers. Paul's brother, Steve, spoke affectionately and well, as did Paul's great golfing friend, Roy Caslon. Alan Dedicoat read beautifully a tribute written by the TOGs. Alan and another of Paul's good friends, Jackie Gill, had organised everything with love and care. Roger Royle led it all with just the right mixture of laughter and nostalgia. The little church was full to bursting with Paul's family, his golfing friends, his musical friends and his colleagues from the BBC. We'd have needed St Paul's to include all the people who wanted to be there, to pay tribute to dear Pauly. I was privileged to deliver the final words:

Paul always said that 'as long as you could still get a four up the first' all would be right with the world. He loved golf, yes, but he loved Mid-Herts more. And how much Mid-Herts GC loved him is evidenced here today, and by the support and care that its members showed Paul during his illness. Whenever we played 'The Captain of Her Heart' on the show, I had to call it 'The Captain of Mid-Herts' – because he was very proud of being the Captain, 'El Capitano'. He played golf as he played life – laconically, gracefully, good-humouredly, and well. You had to dig very deeply to find anything that he took seriously. One of the great popular music producers in modern radio history, he'd push praise aside with the casual 'The music is only important when it's wrong.' He was wrong, but he didn't really believe that anyway – that was his style. It was his life, music, and he continued to pick the music for 'Wake Up To Wogan' until the day he died.

We knew each other a long time. He produced my morning show for a couple of years in the early Eighties, and then, in my second incarnation, for the last ten, lovely years. I don't like disembodied voices on the radio, which is why Alan Dedicoat, such a caring friend, John Marsh and Fran Godfrey play such a vital role. And, of course, Pauly Walters – poorly – Wally Paultry – Wallington P. Magillicuddy de Winter Walters – Doctor Wally, which was how the public best loved him. One morning, he trotted out the old Tony Hancock line: 'Are you a doctor then? No, I never really bothered.' From then on, particularly after I got my Honorary Doctorate, every morning was unremarkable for the same old routine: 'Morning, doctor.' 'Morning, doctor.' 'Pop up on the couch will you, my dear?' 'This may sting a bit' and 'Oh doctor, what are you going to do with that?' 'I'm going to open a window.' Speaking of that old gag, the high spot of Dr Wally's radio stardom was when he broke wind on air, as I was speaking. No one spoke after that for about five minutes. He was voices off, throw-away lines, never intrusive – and over the years, the listening public grew to love him for it. The extraordinary outpouring of grief when they heard of Paul's death bears witness to that love. I've always said that, for a communicator, radio is the superior medium – only on radio can you literally touch the public. Thousands and thousands of people who'd never met him, didn't know what he looked like, grieved and were touched by his passing.

The websites were choked with tributes, the emails in their thousands, the cards and letters that are still coming in. Paul Walters was loved. Loved by everyone who knew him. He wanted you to love him – particularly if you were a woman. He'd never admit it, but he was the world's biggest flirt. He gave every woman in the room the eye – and they loved him for it.

We travelled the world together, Pauly and me. Doonbeg, Champagne, Aberdeen and whatever part of the world is covered by the Eurovision Song Contest along with Paul's friend and mine, Ken Bruce. And I'd like here and now to stamp out the rumour that we were drunk when we did the Contest. We had an iron rule: none of us touched a drop before the fifth song. It took some willpower . . .

But no matter where Paul travelled, he never really left

home. Kimpton, Harpenden, Gustard Wood, Mid-Herts – he
was born, raised and lived here, all his far-too-short life. He
thought of himself as a good old country boy; not British,
English – Anglo-Saxon with a touch of Viking.

He was handsome, he was witty, he was gentle, he was
kind, he had good ears, and he was a great putter. He always
said that his epitaph would be 'Forgotten, but not gone.' How
wrong he was . . .

As we say in Gaelic: Nior fhaichimid a leitheid aris. We'll not
see his like again.

3 November 2006

The great fireworks display is one of the highlights of the
'Wake Up To Wogan' year on Radio 2. Possibly the greatest
display ever not seen, it hasn't been heard from Beijing to
Toronto, from Woolomoloo to Malibu, from Dubai to the
Land of the Long White Cloud. From all over the world come
letters of appreciation and sheer amazement at the virtual
colour, beauty and spectacle of this two-hour extravaganza.
And most wonderful of all, there are no bangs, explosions, nor
the slightest sound to frighten the kiddies or, more importantly, the animals. Or so I thought . . .

I must take you to task over your statement that your fire-
works display does not frighten animals.

My border collie, Pepper, has just heard you mention fire-
works and is now cowering under the bed with her paws over

her ears, in memory of the last time you had a display.

Your fireworks may not be audible to human ears, but to a dog with remarkable hearing like Pepper, they are still a frightening experience. Perhaps you could ask the electronic wizards at the BBC to put a high-band filter on your programme on the day of the fireworks display to ensure that all noise is suppressed.

Thanks.

RICHARD

Fireworks

Naturally, Health and Safety jumped on the 'virtual' bandwagon.

*I thought you'd be pleased to know that the idea of virtual
Guy Fawkes celebrations is catching on. Here in Ilfracombe
this year we are to have a virtual bonfire!! Much safer, but
I'm not sure how you cook your spuds on it.*

> *Hoorah Hooray,*
> *Soon comes the day*
> *When fireworks fill the air,*
> *With super flashes*
> *And rocket dashes,*
> *And sparkle everywhere.*
> *And those that flow*
> *From Wogan's show*
> *Are super safe and pleasing,*
> *With all the joys,*
> *But with no noise*
> *(Apart from Wogan wheezing).*

KATIE MALLETT

The usual suspects flung themselves in with their customary
abandon:

> *There's an annual firework display*
> *For everyone to see*
> *Without the fizzes and the bangs*
> *Held on the BBC*
> *There's Wogan's mighty Whizzer*
> *And Boydies Banger in blue*
> *King Deadly's Dancing Daredevil*
> *And Franny's Fizzer too*
> *But Boggy's Bursting Bombshell*

Just went phut and plib
It was not so much a bombshell
More like an old damp squib.

WILTING

As ever, there's no pleasing everybody . . .

I am attending the firework display and I'm afraid that I
must complain about the lack of arrangements that have been
made for the general public.

For example: where can I park? There appear to be no signs
up anywhere to inform me of this, and while I'm at it, are
there any catering facilities on site? I have a car full of kids,
none of them having had any breakfast yet and they're getting
uglier by the minute; their tempers aren't improving either
come to think of it.

These things really need more thinking through you know.
Free displays are one thing but without all the extras you'd be
better not to bother in my opinion.

BEA GRUDGERY

4 November 2006

It's hard to blame the Old Geezers and Gals from growing a
mite testy, when 'research shows' that global warming is set to
turn this old world of ours into a blasted, barren rock with
nothing but pestilence, floods and famine in prospect. And it's
all our fault. Our generation is leaving this terrible legacy for
the unfortunate next generation. Then, in the same breath, we

are told that this following generation is among the most violent, drunken, yobbish and promiscuous in Europe. It's enough to make a TOG jump into his 4x4 and rev it for a couple of hours. Let's see how those hoodies fend off the acid rain . . .

6 November 2006

Bad news for Jamie Oliver. It now appears the kiddies are being put off school dinners by his Healthy Eating menu. Remember how Number 10, as ever obsessed with the chance of a quick headline, jumped on Jamie's bandwagon and slavishly agreed to throw out the turkey twizzler in favour of more nutritious fare? Now the backlash: mothers are turning up at the school gates with hamburgers and bacon butties to try to stave off the hunger pangs of their starving children, who are not responding as Jamie and Tony might have hoped, to carrot, coriander and broccoli bake:

> So, dear old Jamie Oliver says that because our kids are all bloaters, they can't have pie and chips any more, instead they now have delights such as 'broccoli and tofu surprise'. Of course, the only surprise is that the little blighters don't want to eat it, and now the school dinner system is about to go into meltdown. All the government needed to do was look at a fine figure of a muscleman you turned out to be, on a diet of snorkers and the odd glass of the black stuff! Healthy eating? Pah!
>
> Listening to your news boy this morning talking about the school children being put off school dinners by the healthy

eating menu, I could not agree more, it was being brought up on treacle pudding, spotted dick, runny jelly, lumpy gravy and bullet peas that made us the TOGs we are. Feed them proper food for heaven's sake or we will end up with a new generation of weaklings.

L. OLLIEPOP

7 November 2006

The television schedules are alive with cooking shows: Gordon, Nigella, Antony, Ainsley, John, Richard, Rick – and now, the man whose Fat Duck restaurant has been voted the 'best in the world', Heston Blumenthal. Heston's a far cry from turkey twizzlers and, if it comes to that, broccoli and tofu surprise. Heston's idea, if I've grasped the concept, is to make everything taste differently from how it looks: an orange-coloured slice tastes of beetroot, a slice of what looks like beetroot tastes of orange. Bacon and egg ice cream, snail porridge. Naturally, notwithstanding that we're up to our shoulder-pads in chefs and cooks of every description, Heston must have his own show. After a couple of episodes, the general consensus is that it's been, well, different. Different, in the sense that what old Hest is doing bears not the slightest relation to the efforts of the ordinary man and woman in the kitchen. Hest is on another planet, cookingwise. He wants a chicken – he goes to France to buy it . . .

Chelsea, Miss Barracks, writes from Teignmouth:

Doubtless I am not the only TOG who sat transfixed last night watching Esther Bloomingdale, owner of The Fast Buck restaurant in Bray, striving to create the perfect Black Forest Gateau using only a vacuum cleaner and a paint sprayer and roller. Inspirational stuff, as I found later, when I set about my own modest offering of 'Cauliflower au fromage avec les saucissons de Lincolnshire' with a blowtorch and some turps.

I understand that Esther has been awarded no less than three Michelin tyres, which, in my book, makes him one short of a full set.

8 November 2006

Yesterday morning at about 6.20, as I made my way to my gainful employment through the dark, leafless, damp lanes of South Bucks, a vehicle swept by my car in what can only be described as an unseemly rush. What caught the eye was that it was a milk float, and I didn't think that they could go that fast. I didn't have long to wonder what the rush was, as a police car shot by, lights flashing, in swift pursuit. Down the dark lanes they surged in front of me, the milk float refusing to pull over, the police car blazing. After a mile or two of hell-for-leather chasing, the milk float swerved up a narrow track into the trees, the police car followed, and I saw them no more. It brought cheer and colour to what otherwise might have been another dreary November morn, and I could hardly wait to regale my listeners with the bizarre tale of the runaway milk float. What, I speculated, was the story behind the chase? What was the outcome? Who'd steal a milk float as a getaway vehicle?

Express Dairies

The listeners leapt upon the story like ravening wolves:

The fleeing milk float was obviously Sam the herdsman from
The Archers, *distraught from Ruth's rejection of him at 7.13*
p.m. last night. He's taken his revenge, left the Brookfield
Farm milking parlour a smoking ruin, shut Bert in the
orchard tree house and let the cows out on to the Grey Gables
golf course.

FROM KAREN IN DEEPEST EAST WILTSHIRE

In case you've forgotten, *The Archers* has transmogrified from
an everyday story of country-folk into a hotbed of illicit
goings-on behind the cowshed. Then, Ernie – remember?, the
fastest milkman in the west – dropped me a line that cleared
things up nicely:

Thank you for getting out of the way this morning as I was
on the way to make my special delivery of fresh yoghurt to

Highgrove this morning. The police escort was to make sure that I got there on time for HRH's breakfast.

You don't get fresher yoghurt and cheese anywhere else, and the 200-mile journey along English country lanes at a constant 60 mph from the Duchy is just perfect for the processing.

Book early for Christmas, to be sure of your order.

Actually, the truth was a tad more mundane: a couple of likely lads, one hour ahead of the posse, jumped into the milk float as the milkman was delivering a couple of pints of semi-skimmed, the police gave chase, and it all ended in a field near Slough, with one miscreant apprehended, and the other making his escape. They'll probably get off with a caution, but I'd like to think there'll always be a job for them with Express Dairies . . .

10 November 2006

A week to go to the big *Children in Need* night . . . Can we do better than last year? We make a rod for our own backs every year – each time, it has to be bigger and better than the previous one. Last year, by way of a trailer, a very clever film was made of me, break-dancing; all the moves, spinning on the head, in front of an admiring crowd of young clubbers. It went down well, got a great reaction from the public and helped their awareness that *Children in Need* was happening. What to do this year? How could we top that? Well, they did. Just as last year they put my head on a rapper's body, this time they have my face on the shoulders of someone with a body like Arnold

Schwarzenegger, all bulging muscles and twitching pecs. We filmed it a couple of weeks ago in an underground car park, supposedly an illegal bare-knuckle bout. Great fun to shoot, with lots of well-known television faces in the crowd, and blow me down, if the reaction I'm getting is anything to go by, it's going to be even more successful than last year:

> *The other evening my family and I sat down in front of the television to enjoy our early evening meal when your* Children in Need *trailer appeared. The sight of your pulsating pecs and bulging biceps made us lose our appetites for the tripe and onions we were just tucking into. In future can we have a three-minute warning prior to transmission so that we can avert our gaze and also have enough time to muzzle the dog?*
>
> MOLLY CODDLIN

On the other hand . . .

> *Oy, Wogan, you've done it again . . . confusing old people seems to be your forte! A couple of nights ago the wife and I had my 86-year-old nan round for dinner. It was a lovely meal and soon after we settled down to watch an hour or two of TV. It wasn't long before you popped up on the screen. However, this time it was for a worthy cause – you weren't touting a DVD or hawking the Radio 2 DJ's 'pop-up' book.*
>
> *No, it was the trailer for this year's* Children in Need *show.*
>
> *I could hardly believe my eyes when you whipped your shirt off and revealed that Adonis-like torso; very impressive, I must say.*
>
> *Just at that moment I happened to glance over at my nan and saw a couple of tears welling up in her eyes.*

At first I thought it must have been her bunions playing up. 'All right, Nan?' I asked. 'Ooh yes, I've not seen this fellah for a long time, not since Hughie Green's show in the Sixties . . . lovely. Is he gonna make 'em dance?' she asked. Both myself and my wife were a bit dumbfounded. 'It's that Tony Holland from Opportunity Knocks,' *she shouted, 'that's him. Is he gonna make all them muscles dance?'*

The penny finally dropped and I had to explain this wasn't the guy she thought it was. She looked quite disappointed when I told her, 'It's Terry Wogan, Nan.' 'Ooh dear, I don't think he'll make 'em dance,' she said, 'but what a lovely man, very brave. He spent two years tied to a radiator in Beirut, you know . . . lovely man, lovely man.'

It left me wondering just how many other people up and down the country wouldn't know you from a contortionist clergyman. Bless them, I didn't have the heart to tell her who you actually were.

REG PLAIT

And, as ever, my old mucker, Baz of Wilts, couldn't resist his Lewis Carroll urges:

'You are old father Wogan,' the young man said,
'And your hair has turned grey, all the more so
'And yet you insist on sticking your head
'Upon some other person's grand torso.'

'In my youth,' replied Wogan, 'I'd go to the gym
'And my body looked ever like that
'But now, Sonny Jim, I'm not quite so slim
'In fact some would say I look fat.'

'You are old,' said the youth, 'so do tell us the truth.
'Is it really your frame that we see?
'For I'm sure at your age, you are well past the stage
'Where you're looking as fit as a flea.'

'In my youth,' said the sage, 'when I was your age
'I would exercise daily instead
'So the torso you see, well it really is me
'But I don't think you'll find it's my head!'

18 November 2006

The dust has settled, the captains and the kings departed, and last night's *Children in Need* spectacular realised £18.3 million in seven hours of live television, comfortably beating last year's record of £17 million. I don't have to stick my neck out very far, or slip into my Nostradamus cloak, to confidently predict that we'll be distributing over £30 million next year to little children's charities all over the country desperately in need of help.

I'm so proud of this wonderful work, so privileged to have been part of it since the beginning. And so very, very proud of my loyal TOGs, who have raised millions over the years. This year, with their unpaid, unsung selflessness, they have raised over £1 million with sales of the *Janet and John* CD. It'll still be selling next year so, by the time the last one is packaged and posted by Helen Back, Norm, Dora Jarr, Edina Cloud and all my other heroes and heroines, the total will be closer to £1.5 million. Then there's the TOGs calendar: £120,000 when I last looked . . .

From Monday to Thursday this week on Radio 2, from eight o'clock until quarter to nine, along with Paul Viney and his mighty gavel, I've been auctioning 'things that money can't buy'. Once again, last year's record-breaking total of £300,000 was shattered by the generosity of my listeners, over half a million pounds raised in four mornings over only three-quarters of an hour . . . It's humbling, and it's heartening – the best thing I ever have done, or ever will do, on television or radio.

22 November 2006

Just when you think they've nodded off again at Number 10, evidence emerges that the government is determined to be ruthless in its pursuit of Tony's promise to be 'tough on crime, tough on the causes of crime'. A new gadget is to be introduced that will enable the police to take fingerprint impressions from motorists and other wrongdoers. These fingerprints will, within a scant five minutes, be connected to a database, which, in turn, will instantly check to see if the mugger, thief, rapist (but mainly, motorist) has, as they say in the Yard, 'previous'. There's only one, tiny catch: the fingerprints can only be taken if the wrongdoer gives permission. We can all sleep safe in our beds . . .

23 November 2006

A decent man named Bob Frapples, from Sheffield (we've already established, I hope, that nobody ever writes to me under their real name – the shame would be too great . . .), notices that 'they' sneaked in the news item about the government hoping to raise the retiring age under the cover of darkness. Bob says they're aiming for a retiring age of sixty-eight-plus by 2046. He'll be eighty-two by then, so hopefully will only be eligible for light yard duties. Although they'll probably have a tax for that by then. In common with the rest of us rapidly declining Old Geezers and Gals, it appears that our fears, fuelled by films such as *Logan's Run*, where the over-thirties were surplus to requirements and disposed of, or *Soylent Green*, where the over-forties were similarly dispatched, were unfounded. Here's to retirement at ninety and a free hoverboard pass.

25 November 2006

In the wake of the annihilation of England's cricketers, whitewashed to death in every Test by Australia, today I received this salutary tale from Down Under.

In an effort to relieve the tedium of her classroom, a teacher asks each of her little horrors what their fathers do for a living. The answers are predictable: builder, doctor, factory worker, policeman, etc. However, one little chap appears reluctant to divulge the required information. The teacher persists, and eventually the lad admits: 'My father wears make-up and a Tarzan outfit, and entertains women at parties, where they tear off his spangled posing-pouch.' At the end of the lesson, the teacher keeps the little fellow behind. 'Now then,' she says kindly, 'does your father really do that for a living?' 'No,' says the boy, 'he plays cricket for England, but I was too ashamed to tell you.'

Each post brings its share of suggestions as to the next move for England's cricketers, like this, from a concerned Scot: 'After the success of Darren Gough, and recently Mark Ramprakash, on *Strictly Come Dancing*, could not the BBC run a competition to seek new cricketing talent among professional ballroom dancers?'

1 December 2006

Winter's here, it's been raining since September, but you can still be prosecuted for watering your hardy annuals.

Here comes Rod Eddington, former chairman of the world's favourite airline. And if I may digress – and why wouldn't I? – an airline without much of a clue how to win friends and influence people. Quite the reverse, with their system of rewarding frequent flyers. Fly with them a lot, they'll give you a blue card. This allows you to sit in a lounge. Fly a bit more, they'll give you a silver one. This allows you to jump a queue, and sit in the same lounge. Fly with BA every week, and they'll send you a gold card. This allows you to jump the queue, and sit in the first-class lounge. Hurrah, you think, I've made it! Comfort at last. But not, unfortunately, forever. Fly a little less than you did last year, and they take your gold card away. If for some reason, say ill health or change of job, you fly even more infrequently, they take away your silver card and, in time, your blue card as well. If anybody can work out how this acts as an incentive to fly British Airways, get in touch with Willie Walsh. Oh, and I understand that there's a platinum card as well, but you only get that if you're a friend of the chairman, and it's yours forever – even if you fly Ryanair.

But, if you can be bothered to cast your keen brain back a paragraph, you'll see that I've digressed. The aforementioned Rod Eddington, presumably on the assumption that despite British Airways he knows something about transport, has come up with a report that commends the idea of motorists paying to use the roads, which might be a blinder of an idea if we weren't already paying, through road tax and petrol tax. The bold Rodders wants to use these charges to cut congestion, thereby saving the planet and the whale. It all sits uncomfortably with Rod's previous insistence that we need bigger airports, more and bigger planes, in order to dump lots more carbon emissions into the atmosphere. Can anyone spot the flaw in Rod's argument?

Sky charging

5 December 2006

A news report that some employers are refusing to allow their workplaces to display baubles, tinsel, Christmas trees and the rest of the Yuletide paraphernalia, which has been on show in Harrods and Selfridges since August, is causing an uproar. It has been misconstrued and blown out of all proportion by a knee-jerk reaction that has interpreted it as religious prejudice, a politically correct injunction to prevent Christians celebrating Christmas in the traditional way for fear of offending those with other religious beliefs. Useless to point out that tinsel, baubles and trees have nothing to do with the Christian Christmas message, or that the employers were only acting according to the strictures of Health and Safety, lest someone should trip over a pine needle and immediately contact Injury Lawyers For You ... An outraged listener wrote to say that they had lately returned from Dubai (Islamic) where they had seen a band of animatronic teddy bears in Santa outfits performing Christmas songs and carols. That's all right, then.

8 December 2006

To the New Forest – or more specifically, the Chewton Glen Hotel. Easy enough to find if you follow the hotel's own directions closely. If, however, you leave it to the car's SatNav, you find yourself in the outskirts of Bournemouth. Here's a little tip: never ask your car's satellite navigation unit to direct you to your destination by the 'quickest' route. It'll take you to the nearest motorway, no matter how far it is out of your way. A couple of years ago, it found me in Shepton Mallet, and the following day I foolishly asked it for the quickest way to an address in Devon. It took me back to Bristol, whence I had come, then the M4, M5 – but you know the rest, if you know the region. Five hours later, having described a complete semi-circle, we found ourselves at our destination. Well, when I say our destination, I mean a gate in a dark country lane. When we eventually found the hotel we were looking for, the manager smiled ruefully, and said, 'Oh, it's always doing that . . .'

Anyway, we're in Chewton Glen because it's where we and the rest of the family – Mark and Susan, baby Harry, Katherine, Henry and baby Freddie, my niece Jane and husband Richie from New York, and various Bensons, Ulfanes and diverse friends – are staying for Alan and Kate's wedding tomorrow. Yes, Alan Wogan's getting married! I can't say that without feeling that there should be a 21-gun salute. He's kept his mother waiting all these years. We've always said that Alan was content to wait until some beautiful creature sneaked up on him from behind, knocked him over the head and dragged him off to her lair. Then he met Kate Slade, and the writing was on the wall for Wogan's oldest bachelor. They're to be married tomorrow, at Boldre Church, near Sway, where the Slades have a lovely house, and great marquees have been set up for the celebrations. We thought we'd better find Boldre Church, in view of the fact that they were expecting us for the rehearsal of the wedding. We found it, much as we had found Chewton Glen, after a great deal of up-hill and down-daleing. My mood wasn't improved when the vicar said, 'Better late than never!' as we entered. I'm convinced half the guests will never find this place . . .

We all gather for a Slade/Wogan dinner in the evening at the hotel. Mike Slade is a wonderful, generous host, the food and the wine splendid, and Kate, since, traditionally, she won't speak at the wedding reception, speaks lovingly and charmingly of her family and her love for Alan. Mark and Susan Wogan's new baby, Harry, sleeps throughout it all, by the table.

9 December 2006

The sun shines through the windows of our room; it's a lovely December day for the last Wogan wedding. It's in the late afternoon, so we have plenty of time for a glass of champagne, and the 'ushers' lunch', a tradition that they didn't have in my day, unfortunately. A cheery occasion, hosted by Alan, with good wine and the leg of a duck to stave off any hunger pangs that might assail us in the church. It sets the tone for what turns out to be a wonderful, joyous day. I can't believe it – everyone's found the church! Even the rellies from Dublin, the West of Ireland, America and Australia. I must find out where they got their SatNavs . . . The vicar, Camilla Walton, has been really helpful, and generously allowed Revd Roger Royle and Father Brian D'Arcy to interfere, as they have for all Wogan weddings. In the words of an old Radio 2 hit, 'Love is Everywhere', Mike Slade fights back the tears as he leads his beautiful Kate up to the altar. Readings, blessings and, during the signing of the register, a brilliant soprano, Diana Montague, sings. When she finishes there is silence, except for from the second pew, where my two-year-old grandson, Freddie Cripps, claps his hands, and shouts 'Hooray!' In an unforgettable wedding, on an unforgettable day, it's a memory I shall carry to the grave.

The reception is simply magnificent – one marquee brightly lit, replete with a caviar bar, an oyster bar and a slice of Jabugo ham to go with your pink champagne. The other marquee is lit by candles and little individual lanterns that each guest carries to their table. A perfect evening of wonderful wine and food, and funny, touching speeches by Mike, Alan and Mark. Then the curtain rolls back, and a 21-piece band strikes up. The dancing goes on, enhanced by a lively cocktail bar, until the wee small hours, when Alan and Kate leave, fireworks lighting their way. Thanks to Mike and Heather Slade, a day to look back on through the years with a smile.

15 December 2006

The débâcle that is the England cricket team's tour of Australia continues to cause real pain, but, as always in the case of my listeners, it's a painful smile:

I hear on the news this morning that the England cricket chaps have managed to lose the Ashes to those colonial types Down Under.

Now I don't pretend to understand anything about cricket, in fact I'm not even sure what the 'Ashes' are, but I have to say I'm most impressed with the fact that former X-Factor winner, Shane Ward, can not only knock out a half-decent tune but is a mean bowler too.

Maybe Simon Cowell can now sort us out a decent rugby

*side for the Six Nations or maybe a footie team capable of
winning the World Cup. Come on Simon – do it for Blighty!*

It helps, I suppose, particularly when there's a kindly word
from north of the border:

*So that's it then. The Ashes have been lost and won, and now
the hurly-burly's done – so what for the future? You do appre-
ciate I hope that we Scots are concerned about the condition
of the England cricket team – we like it when you get into a
position where you can play the braggart, and then get
gubbed.*

Then, I receive this, claiming to come from the wires of
Associated Press, Sydney, Australia:

SYDNEY (AP)

*A seven-year-old boy was at the centre of a Parramatta, NSW,
courtroom drama yesterday when he challenged a court ruling
over who should have custody of him.*

*The boy has a history of being beaten by his parents and the
judge initially awarded custody to his aunt, in keeping with
child custody law and regulations requiring that family unity
be maintained to the degree possible.*

*The boy surprised the court when he proclaimed that his
aunt beat him more than his parents and he adamantly refused
to live with her. When the judge then suggested that he live with
his grandparents, the boy cried out that they also beat him.*

*After considering the remainder of the immediate family
and learning that domestic violence was apparently a way of
life among them, the judge took the unprecedented step of*

allowing the boy to propose who should have custody of him.

After two recesses to check legal references and confer with child welfare officials, the judge granted temporary custody to the English cricket team, whom the boy firmly believes are not capable of beating anyone.

Too close to the truth to be funny . . .

20 December 2006

I love Christmas. Don't give me all that guff about how it's been ruined by over-commercialisation and dysfunctional families and how we've all lost the real spirit of Christmas. Not in my house. We've always had a marvellous time. Helen decks the halls, looks like a queen and cooks like a dream. Everybody spends too much, eats too much and drinks their share. Every year, in my capacity as Father of the Feast and Head of the House, I make a desperate attempt to curtail the conspicuous consumption and demand that there be an end to the excessive present-giving. I am cruelly ignored. We'll see on Christmas Day, but I'm not encouraged by the rising pile of gifts that already looks as if it's going to swamp the Christmas tree. It's Helen's fault. This is a woman who thinks that if you're giving somebody a present, you might as well give them another one – and another – and another . . . You'd think that the children might have taken after their more parsimonious father, but over the years I seem to have caught the bug from my wife and turned into Scrooge post-ghosts. God help us, everyone . . .

25 December 2006

Christmas started with a vengeance last Friday, the 22nd, with a dinner party for our friends the Allisses – how long have I known Peter, Jackie and their family? Also the Jacobs – God, we have known Catherine even longer, since she was a model in Dublin with Helen – the Ulfanes, with whom we're going to spend the New Year in Italy, and Jim Sherwood, whose wife Shirley is too ill to come. We toasted her return to rude good health. To give Helen a break from the endless cooking of Christmas, we got the chef from Katherine and Henry's pub brasserie, the Greene Oak, near Windsor, to cook for us. One of the few dinner parties we've had where Helen is not springing up and down like a bee's wing, as dear departed Pauly Walters used to say. We'll miss him on Boxing Day; he always came for dinner and stayed the night. King Deadly, Voice of the Balls, Wealdstone Wonder is keeping old Pauly's seat warm this year. A jolly, kindly soul, who eats for three.

Today, as is traditional, we start with scrambled eggs, smoked salmon and champagne. Then, we open the presents. It takes about three hours; as usual, nobody has paid the slightest notice to my words of caution, and there's even more parcels and packages, with grandchildren Freddie and Harry. We miss Alan and Kate, still on honeymoon – they came back from the Maldives and immediately took off for the ski slopes of Megève. The turkey is moist and magnificent, with the crispy skin that is the only thing that actually makes it worth eating. It's a big boring bird, and I knew too many of those in my youth . . .

Years ago, when the children were much younger, Helen proposed that we enjoy more interesting fowl on Christmas Day, such as duck. The kids were appalled – we were throwing their beloved traditions out of the window. You know, I think they'd still be the same today.

In the good old days, I'd eat so much that I'd have to lie on the floor after, and sometimes during, dinner. Now, I don't even try to move from my chair.

Our great friends Bev and Liz were with us for lunch on Christmas Eve, and tomorrow Helen's at the oven and wielding the skillet again. Deadly's joining us for Boxing Day

Wogan Christmas

dinner with Ray and Sylvia, whom we first met over thirty years ago, when we were all river-folk by the Thames at Bray. We moved from there shortly after the Parkinsons moved in, knowing that property values would drop.

Did I mention that I love Christmas? I think Helen does too, but I don't want to disturb her – she's lying down in a darkened room.

28 December 2006

Off to Heathrow Terminal One for our flight to Rome. We're spending a few days there and welcoming the New Year in with our friends Max and Joy, who have a magnificent *castello* in Fighine, a tiny hilltop hamlet near Orvieto, with stunning views across Umbria to Lake Trasimeno and Perugia.

I never approach Rome Airport with anything other than trepidation, but it's relatively painless this time, apart from the usual delays in the baggage hall. The trip up the spine of Italy can be horrendous, but today we're in Fighine in an hour and three-quarters. The castle and the hamlet's houses have been sensitively and beautifully restored by David Mlinaric, and the Italianate garden is white with roses.

31 December 2006

After a traditional Italian New Year's Eve dinner of *bollito misto*, mixed boiled meats, and Max's impeccable choice of

Italian wines, as the clock strikes midnight he invites his guests to a splendid fireworks display. We gather, beverages in hand, on the castle's terrace, and on a chill New Year's night, all of Italy is lit up. Every little village, every town for miles is staging its own fireworks extravaganza. Away to the south, towards Orvieto, to the north, towards Cortona, past Perugia, the rockets and starbursts rise, blaze into riotous colour and fall. It seems to go on for hours. And only the cold drives us indoors to ring the family and wish everybody a Happy New Year. Who knows, intones the old philosopher, what the next twelve months will hold for all of us? Whatever it is, good or bad, we'll enjoy or endure.

3 January 2007

Back to the coalface, and the heartening news of a glamour tip passed on by top fashion photographers to supermodels who don't wish to Botox their way to a Trout Pout. 'Maximise your lips. To pout beautifully, try turning to the camera, and saying "Wogan".' It cheers an Old Geezer up to think that he is on the lips of Kate, Giselle or Kirsty.

'A moment on the lips, forever on the hips.' No, not about Wogan, it's the vittels that do the damage. However, kindly old Nanny Government, pursuant to its *Catcher in the Rye* policy of not allowing any citizen, large or small, to get as much as a smut in their eye, has formulated a system whereby all the food we purchase will be categorised like traffic lights: green for good, amber for 'mind how you go' and red for 'on your own head be it'. A listener tells me that his wife is no Nigella

Lawson of the skillet, so, to help her out in her culinary efforts, he has followed the government's guidelines, by erecting a set of traffic lights in the kitchen. Green will be for acceptable, one more portion please; amber means 'I'm so hungry, I'll eat it anyway'; red can only be translated as 'revolting, give it to the dog'.

Someone else wrote to me today on the subject of food, recounting his wife's irritating habit of saying, 'No, I won't have anything,' when he offers to buy, say, two portions of fish and chips for their evening meal. Then, when he returns with his supper, she spends her time stealing his chips, and the tastiest pieces of fish. If the reaction of my other listeners is anything to go by, this is a widespread feminine ruse:

Many years ago my good lady wife and I were being driven to Cheltenham by a friend. Stopping off for fish and chips en route our friend paid for each of us to have a can of a well-known soft drink. This didn't prevent my wife from asking for a sip of someone else's drink! She didn't want to open hers as it

Fish and chips

would be a waste, her not wanting to drink a whole can. My
friend was flabbergasted – he'd bought her a can of her own
to ward that very comment off. You can't beat them you know.
(There's a law against it apparently.)

And the formidable Clodagh Rubbish draws us a pen-
picture of family life in the Village of the Damned:

Hear hear to yer man with the missus muggin' him for his
chips. I'm with him all the way.
   I myself have been known to be driven to fury and
apoplexy whilst on the business end of a bacon butty with the
daughter Polly beside me, behavin' like one of them baby birds
you see in late spring, flappin' its wings and roarin' at the
poor mother bird as it forages for food to shove down its gullet.
The ensuing fistfights have been spectacular and often end
only with the said daughter administering the Half Nelson
and Stranglehold used so effectively by her late Great-
Grandfather during his bouts with Mick McManus, and
with the aforementioned butty being forcibly extracted from
down me bra.

It's just another little brick in the wall that Health and Safety
wish to build around us all lest we graze our knees. One of my
correspondents tells me that after a delicious meal in the leafy
suburb of Banstead, Surrey, he requested a toothpick, the better to free the last remaining scrap of food from his ill-fitting
dentures and get full value for his money. 'Sorry,' said the wait-
ress, 'we're not allowed to provide them any more, they might
be used as weapons.'

The fog that engulfed Heathrow and Gatwick at the end of December ruined thousands of would-be travellers' holidays and is still creating chaos. Bags that were checked in for flights that never took off are still piled high in the baggage halls of the airport, full of Christmas gifts that were never delivered and holiday clothes that were never worn. As I write, that was nearly two weeks ago. I saw it all as I came into Heathrow a couple of days ago: huge piles of luggage sitting forlornly on trolleys, leaning drunkenly against walls, making the stress of airline travel even more of a nightmare. No need for the doomsayers of global warming to make us all feel guilty about taking to the air; airports have become anathema to pleasurable travel: grim, stressful, unsmiling, overcrowded, and the new security restrictions have made them virtually unbearable. And they're building bigger planes . . .

9 January 2007

The performance of the English cricket team during the Ashes series in Australia still nags at the very vitals of the Englishman, particularly Des Custard, of Tunbridge Wells:

I was reading an article yesterday which suggested that the presence of players' wives, girlfriends and children on overseas tours could be a major distraction for our footballers and cricketers, preventing the lads from bonding as a team and concentrating on the job of winning. I suppose the idea is that their presence adds stability to the players' lives, in the same

*way that 'proper English food' is provided for all the players'
meals.*

*The fear must be that if the players sampled the local food,
or the local women, they might get the runs or catch something – although in the case of England's cricketers, that
might not be a bad thing.*

At the very heart of it all is still the old distrust of Johnny
Foreigner and his low-cunning non-British ways. The French,
of course, are the worst of all. Many people agreed to the
Channel Tunnel only because they thought that it was one-
way, and were aggrieved to find that it allowed the French to
come over to Blighty. Picture then the bemusement that greeted the release into the public domain of hitherto secret
government papers that revealed that in the 1950s the French
premier, Guy Mollet, thought that it might be a *bonne idée* if
France joined the British Commonwealth and the *Entente
Cordiale* became a binding political unity. What became of this
grand plan is not clear; perhaps Anthony Eden was trimming
his elegant moustache at the time and missed it, as he seems to
have missed a great deal, but a true-blue Brit, Eddie Fiss, spoke
for many:

*Sacred Blue! Are my oreilles deceiving me? Imagine the results
of this incroyable proposition! Cricket on the Champs Elysées,
boules in Barnsley, garlic with your poisson and frites, a
pint of vin rouge on a Dimanche lunchtime down the pub,
Spotted Dick at the Tour d'Argent – it is all too 'orrible to
contemplate. But maybe we would have trains that ran on
time and three-hour lunches. Did we miss an opportunity
perhaps?*

15 January 2007

The BBC officially said farewell to our dear Pauly Walters today, with a reception in the Council Chamber of Broadcasting House. All put together beautifully by the person who, more than anyone else, stood by Paul in his darkest hours: Alan Dedicoat, Voice of the Balls, Wealdstone Weatherboy, habitué of the Northolt Swimerama. All Pauly's friends from the BBC, the music business and Mid-Herts Golf Club who couldn't squeeze into the church on that sad day in November were there, under the very portrait of Lord Reith where Paul had upset a tray of chipolatas a few years before and had found himself suddenly alone in a crowded room. I threw a chipolata at his Lordship, in memory of an occasion that always made us laugh. It's always the little things, the inconsequential, that trip the memory cells and bring back the smile – and the tear.

There were TOGs there today, and they were crying. Paul was the link between them and me; he took their letters, and replied to them. He was their friend, one of them, and they loved him. But Katie Melua sang, and the mood, as it had been in church, was of joy, the celebration of a lovely man who had enriched us all with his presence.

18 January 2007

Recording of the third series of *Wogan, Now and Then* starts today at BBC Television Centre, the sad old Deserted

Doughnut. Those of us who remember the days when the place bustled with activity, bursting with ideas, talent, programmes literally pouring from the busy studios, find it a sad place now: dishevelled, listless, kept alive by independent productions such as mine and Paul O'Grady's. Mind you, they have dolled up a couple of the dressing rooms with settees and sofas, a huge television in the middle of the room, and two more, one in the bathroom, and the other in a dark corner by a lounger. There are tables and chairs, a fridge and a space about a foot wide in which to hang up your clothes. Bring me the head of the interior designer ... On the other hand, nobody would want to spend longer than a couple of minutes in the old dressing rooms. For years, on *Children in Need* night, I was squashed into a tiny, dingy space with two chairs and a filthy carpet, an old pot of coffee and some curled-up sandwiches. The not such good old days ...

We record two shows, one at two-thirty in the afternoon and the second at five. Two packed audiences and, I hope, two good shows. It's such fun to work with Quentin as floor manager and Stu as director. It's an old pals' reunion; we all worked together for years on *Children in Need*. Spun Gold TV is the show's producer and a joy – relaxed, professional, full of good ideas. The broadcaster, UK TV Gold, with Diane Howie at the helm, is supportive and happy with what's going on.

On Show One, three people whom I've interviewed in the dim and distant – Leo Sayer, Jane Seymour and Leslie Phillips. Leo has just survived *Big Brother* without much visible scarring. Jane is extraordinary: flawlessly beautiful, unchanged from twenty years ago. Leslie, of the long-drawn-out, lascivious 'Hellooo' and the devilish 'Ding Dong!', is another without a crease on his baby-like cheeks. He's just co-starred in the hit movie *Venus* with Peter O'Toole, and is picking up awards like confetti for his performance. He completely denies being a cad, and claims that his posh accent is a fake. Natalie Cassidy, Sonia from *EastEnders*, is the one that I haven't met before. She has just left the show, which she has been doing for fourteen years, since she was ten!

Show Two has Wendy Richards and Jan Leeming as the old stagers, bless 'em. Jan is another reality show survivor, having distinguished herself amidst all manner of creepy-crawlies, most of them human. Jan's been married several times, but the fault seems to have always been with the chaps. I remind her of when she introduced the Eurovision Song Contest in Harrogate. My dearest memory of that is a dinner, the night before the Contest, attended by the chairman of the BBC, George Howard of Castle Howard. He fell asleep into the soup.

Wendy Richards, who has just left *EastEnders*, and makes no bones about the fact that she left because of the direction in which her character had been taken, was in the very first edition of the soap, and also on the very first *Wogan*, my three-times-a-week talk show that was transmitted live from the TV Theatre, Shepherd's Bush Green . . . Memories . . .

Tracey Emin, the controversial artist, is the person I had not interviewed, or indeed met, before. She and her art get regularly bashed by the press, and sometimes, with her attitude and language, she does nothing to worm her way into the hearts of the British public, but tonight she is charming, intelligent, and I really like her. Despite herself, she may well be turning into an institution – she's Britain's representative at the Venice Biennale.

20 January 2007

Tony Blair clings to the wreckage. The man who was set to be Britain's Jack Kennedy, leading us to the sunlit uplands of prosperity, law and order, education and NHS, and a country where everything worked the way it should. And everything is in the same old mess as it was when the *Wunderkind* of New Labour took over. No, it's worse – worse for law and order, for education, for the elderly, for pensions, for transport and most of all for the great Labour dream, Nye Bevin's love-child, the NHS. Polly Filla writes:

> *I was summoned to my GP yesterday: I had ignored a letter instructing me to come for a routine blood test, so the Practice Nurse had telephoned me. I explained that I had absolutely no symptoms, was feeling absolutely fine and didn't have time, but she wasn't having any of it, so yesterday I turned up. She apologised and said, 'I know you don't need this test – but we have to do it.' When I remarked that it must cost them quite a lot of money, she said, 'Oh yes, it does – but you see, if we don't do it, we don't get paid!'*
>
> *I was recently referred for a hospital appointment, and lo and behold I was offered a choice of hospitals in the area. As if I would know which was the best?*
>
> *Even better, though, shortly afterwards I was sent a survey form to complete. The survey, it seems, was commissioned by the NHS to 'monitor people's experience' when arranging a hospital appointment – and my experience will 'help them improve their service'.*
>
> *The form wanted to know was I offered a choice? How did*

I feel about the process of choosing? What three things would be important in choosing a hospital?

Obviously someone had overlooked the most important question: Did they make you better?

Still, isn't it refreshing to know public funds are being spent on such useful surveys – instead of being frittered away on patient care.

NHS survey

21 January 2007

Hallelujah, brothers and sisters! Just when you think that your hitherto ratings-busting reality TV show is down to its last gasp, with viewing figures falling like the leaves in autumn, along come the red-tops, closely followed by what likes to think of itself as the 'quality' press, to splash your sad excuse for entertainment all over their front pages. The ratings rise again, phoenix-like, from the ashes. Then, the icing on the cake. Some numpties jump on the *Big Brother* racist taunts bandwagon in the House of Commons, and the BBC, your opposition for goodness sake, drag it screaming into every news bulletin. Apart from Channel 4, the beneficiaries of this carousel of fools will include a faded Bollywood star, who will once again become the toast of old Bombay, and a mouthy chav of no discernible education, intelligence, talent or beauty, Jade Goody, who, once the dust has settled, will, Kate Moss-like, shrug off the cloak of disgrace, to be offered anything she desires. Is Prince Harry free?

Nowadays, celebrity describes some eejit who, despite having demeaned themselves to the lowest degree, is still ejected from the House, the Jungle or the Love Island. Remember those happy bygone days when we used to complain about the television schedules being congested with makeover, gardening, DIY and interior decorating? Now it's 'reality' or, worse, 'celebrity reality'. Have I said this before?? Throw another log on the fire, it'll get worse before it gets better . . .

23 January 2007

The good ship *Napoli* founders off Branscombe beach in Devon, bringing again to the fore the wrecking and scavenging instincts that the natives have obviously inherited from their ancestors. Not just the locals either. The pillagers and plunderers come from far and wide, to rummage among the containers washed up on the beach. The television cameras show them going about their entrepreneurial work like people possessed, rolling away barrels and bundles, packages and bits of machinery, and motorbikes. All of this larceny observed with a kindly, avuncular eye by the local boys in blue. 'But this is robbery,' cries the honest observer. 'How come they're nicking all this stuff under the eyes of the local constabulary?' It turns out the police are unsure where they stand, apart from lolling about the beach, in the matter of Marine Law. And they certainly don't want to be seen abusing the human rights of thieves and robbers.

''Ere, Tel, wanna buy a motorbike or some nappies? Slightly damp and covered in seaweed, but for you, I can do a special price . . .'

'Hi! I just came here onboard crazy ship *Napoli*. Next time, I come by train! I very sick until welding man let me out. I help him push motorbike up beach, and he give me radio! I learn English from your show.'

26 January 2007

The suggestion that our kindly government, having bled the honest citizen dry with all manner of taxes on all manner of pretexts, may reward reformed drug addicts with free food vouchers, brought a letter from a listener who asked if his 73-year-old mother could become a drug addict, please? Although never having taken an illegal substance in her life, she would be willing to give it a go, if she could then give up, have a urine test once a week, and thereby receive food vouchers to supplement her pension, and help towards paying her council tax. The writer wondered if anybody listening had any contacts for drug dealers in her area as, being a law-abiding citizen, his mother had no idea how to go about it.

27 January 2007

Then, flying in the face of climate change, global warming and disappearing cod, a light dusting of snow fell, south of the Watford Gap, a signal for the entire South-East, and its transport system, to fall apart. Hardy folk from 'oop North' scoffed:

Dust know lad, yon southern jessies never fail to amaze us tuff northerners with yer whinging.

So y've got a bit of snow, and y'll be a bit late for canapés afore yer dinner. Dinner . . . it's tea . . .

Yer dun't know yer born you lot. In Fleetwood we dun't mention t'weather unless it's a force 500 gale wi snow four foot deep an't Irish sea is lapping against pot rack.

RINGO DOOM

Oy Wogan, thi soft owd divvil,

Dun't include us up north with all thy southern cringing jessies when a bit o' snow falls on London. Tha might shut darn th'entire south of England every time t'wind blows but we're still waiting for winter up here. It's not go' below minus 6 yet (although a couple o' folks has been seen out wi' a jumper on — must be southern tourists).

We've only had a sprinkling o'snow so t'coat is still in

t'cupboard and won't come out until th'temperature drops another 10 degrees.

Get thi act together lad and stop thi whining.

ARTHUR BOSOMWORTH, NORTHERN CULTURAL ASSOCIATION, HECKMONDWIKE

2 February 2007

A letter from Don E. Gal of Atlantic View, Norwich (not only a pseudonym, but a pseudaddress . . .):

Shock, horror. A birth certificate has been discovered stating that Peter O'Toole was born in Yorkshire and not Connemara as he has claimed.

All we need now is to be told that you were born in Brick Lane or near the Bull Ring in Birmingham.

If so, then not only will Limerick University demand their doctorate back, but I'll be looking for a refund on these books I've purchased.

Will any records held in Limerick go back far enough to substantiate your case?

Little does the poor eejit know that I'm standing on the terrace of Ireland's tallest hotel, in my native city, with a magnificent view of my historic birthplace and the mighty River Shannon, as it flows to the sea, past the docks and the cement factory. Over by the other bank, the former Cleeve's Toffee factory – with that smell I can still remember – and Ferrybank Convent, where I first went to school, and ran off home on my first day, over several busy roads, nearly frightening my poor mother to death. There's the bank by the Sally Gardens, where I walked to Barrington's Pier, and the rowing eights of the Limerick Club, as ever, glide silently by. Looking back to the old city, the new 'Whistling' Bridge, with the first traffic jam I've ever seen in Limerick, then Sarsfield Bridge, which I crossed on my little bike, back and forward from home to school, four times a day. Then the rapids of the unnavigable river, and St John's Castle, as old and unchanged as I left it, fifty-two years ago.

I'm in Limerick to receive the city's Lifetime Achievement Award, to be presented to me by the Taoiseach himself, Ireland's Prime Minister, Bertie Ahern. It's all been organised by Mary Dundon of the Limerick office, in a masterful manner. A couple of hours ago, she picked us up in a stretch limo, and we streaked into the city with a police motorcycle escort clearing the way. I wondered if she'd do the same thing for me every morning on the M40 into London, but she didn't seem keen.

They kindly asked me if I'd like to invite anybody to see me get the works, and, more in hope than anything, I asked if some of the great friends of my youth could be invited. Mary Dundon found them, and they've agreed to come. I can't believe it! There they are: Jim Sexton, Bill Hayes, his sister Mary, Mick Leahy, Gordon Holmes. Like myself, they're older but no wiser, sharing the laughter and the memories. Fifty-two years roll away, I can see in their eyes that they're as pleased to see me as I am them, and it's moving. Bill has travelled from Kilkenny and Mary from Dublin, and the Limerick incumbents, Jim and Mick, have contributed to a little film. I wouldn't call it a tribute . . . Mick remembers an occasion in a Munster Junior Cup game, against our great rivals, Rockwell

College: 'Rockwell had the ball, and their big powerful centre had broken free, and was heading for our try line. Wogan was a prop forward, but for some reason found himself at full-back, the only thing between the Rockwell centre and a try. The alternatives were clear: Wogan could crash-tackle the charging giant, or stand aside. He stood aside.'

Bertie Ahern made a graceful and complimentary speech, following an equally kind one from the Mayor of Limerick, marred only by his reference to my radio show as 'Wake Up, Wogan'. Ahern is known to all as 'Bertie', a man of the people, but it shouldn't be forgotten that Ireland's economic miracle, the easing of the tensions between North and South, the breaking of prejudices between Gaelic and Garrison games, have all taken place on Bertie's watch.

I say my usual ill-chosen few words and am presented with a replica of the Treaty Stone. A broken treaty by the Williamites that caused many an Irish soldier to find his fortune in Europe, a Wogan among them . . . An honour, and an evening I'll always remember with pride.

5 February 2007

Playing right into the hands of the natural enemy of the turkey and its twizzler, Jamie Oliver, comes news that an outbreak of bird flu has broken out all over Bernard Matthews's Bronze Beauties, which will necessitate a visit from the Grim Reaper for thousands of our feathered friends. A premature end for everybody's favourite Christmas bird, and some people are blaming the Hungarian turkey. Somehow, I knew it would be

Johnny Foreigner's fault ... The media has been up to its armpits in the story for days, and, naturally, Radio 2's newshound, Jeremy Vine, has been in the very van of the hunt for truth. Unfortunately, yesterday he mixed up his Matthews with his Mannings:

> *I have emailed you to seek assurance that there is indeed NO outbreak of Bernard Manning in Suffolk, as reported by Jezza Vine in his 'poor man's* Panorama*' lunchtime show yesterday.*
>
> *I still recall the devastation caused by the Les Dawson outbreak in the Seventies, and would like you to be the calming voice of the nation, in assuring us that the government has a strategy in place for further outbreaks of comedians.*
>
> *I cannot even attempt to comprehend the carnage caused by a future outbreak of Ant and Dec.*
>
> *I must be away and board up the windows, then send the wife and kids to higher ground, as we live quite close to Jasper Carrott!!*
>
> TUBULAR MEL
> BIRMINGHAM

7 February 2007

All is uneasy anticipation for the band of wintry conditions that is about to assail Southern Softies. The hardy folk who live north of a line drawn from Birmingham to the Wash may scoff, but south of the Watford Gap we're not used to snow and ice, and the lightest of dustings will undoubtedly bring all rail and road transport to a grinding halt. We have little faith in gritters and their ilk, and there has been bulk-buying on a large scale, as people prepare to dig in and batten down the hatches.

An unlikely correspondent, by the name of Jamie Doughnut, has timely words of warning for those who must make car journeys: drivers should make sure that they are warmly dressed, and avoid shorts and T-shirts, even if they are postmen. The following are vital if the driver is trapped by snowdrifts:

(1) a large shovel

(2) a 100-kilogram bag of sand

(3) a flask containing a hot drink

(4) sufficient food to sustain energy levels

(5) a book to read – Mustn't Grumble *is available at a greatly reduced price at all booksellers*

(6) an exercise device, such as a rowing machine, to maintain muscular tone

(7) a cardboard tube, so drivers can rip off their door mirrors and make a periscope to see above the snow

(8) a set of sweeps' brushes, which will enable drivers to poke a 'help' sign above the surface of the snow

(9) a pack of huskies and a sled.

Wise precautions indeed, but I detect a groundswell of opinion that we should be making the most of the snow. If all those terrible warnings about climate change are true, we'll be battling our way through sandstorms this time next year . . .

8 February 2007

After all that mockery yesterday about severe weather conditions about to bring Soft Southern Jessies to their knees, my chickens, like poor Bernard Matthews's turkeys, came home to roost. Not just mine, but everybody else's. We woke to a carpet of the deep and crisp and even, and since I live on higher ground, a good deal deeper in my case. Yesterday, I shrewdly advised Dennis, my good friend, companion and excellent driver, that we should try to make an earlier start than usual this morning, in case weather conditions turned nasty. So there I am, ready to brave the elements in the name of Radio 2, striding about in my boots, eager for the challenge. Mush! Then Dennis rings. He's stuck at the bottom of the hill, unable to make the ascent in the deep snow. He's tried reversing up the hill, he's tried reversing back to get a run at it, and all he's done is slide gently backwards to where he started! I ring Alan Boyd to tell him I may not make it this morning. He's arrived already, of course, because he lives in London, and the snow has already melted there. Sarah Kennedy, another London resident and Southern Softy, will have to carry the can, which, since she started at five in the morning and mightn't finish until half past nine, will tax her pluck to the limit.

The minutes tick by, the likelihood of my making it microphone-side becomes increasingly unlikely. Someone has given Sarah the good news, I hear her complain that the Victoria sponge she has left in the oven will be ruined. It'll be the soufflés next ... Then, a half an hour later than we'd planned, Dennis, brave, loyal Dennis, bowls up through the drifts. Don't ask me how he's made it, but as far as I'm concerned, he's

Ranulph Twistleton Fiennes. We skid and shuffle our way to the M4, which miraculously has been cleared by the unexpected diligence of the gritters, and I make it to the studio three-quarters of an hour late. And what do I get for my steely determination that the show must go on? A moaning colleague, whose Victoria sponge has collapsed, and eight million listeners who want to know what exactly my game is, turning up this late? I shed a silent tear, and carry on . . .

10 February 2007

Where did I get the quaint notion that the whole idea of the new supercasinos was to revive the flagging fortunes of Blackpool and the hole in the public purse that is the Dome? Manchester's the place! Well, so far . . . You never know with Manchester – the BBC is supposed to be moving chunks of its production there, but nobody in Broadcasting House nor White City really believes it's going to happen. Wishful thinking? The BBC's previous experience, in merely moving its radio news from Regent Street, London, to Wood Lane, West London, proved disastrous, resulting in a return to Regent Street at a cost of hundreds of millions of pounds. The Media and Broadcast Centres of White City echo to footsteps in empty rooms. Will it be even more of a ghost town with the move to Manchester, and the return to Broadcasting House, Portland Place?

We, Terry's Old Geezers and Gals, are hoping that, wherever the supercasino hangs its hat, there'll be a place for the senior citizen: high-stake games of Ludo, Happy Families and

Bridge will keep sporting oldsters happy; however Snap will be ruled out, on the advice of St John's Ambulance, lest tempers flare. Elderly waitresses will serve free cups of tea and late-night cocoa to encourage the older gambler to stay and fritter away even more of their pension on those machines where you try to get precariously balanced coins to tip over the edge, with a possible jackpot of £2.25p. Let the good times roll . . .

11 February 2007

It appears that one of the more endearing anomalies of life in Britain is that the government claim to know the exact location of every untaxed vehicle in Britain, but haven't a clue as to the whereabouts of thousands of illegal immigrants, terrorists, escaped murderers, rapists and paedophiles. The obvious answer is for the Home Office to stand down, and put the DVLA in charge. A further workmanlike suggestion from a listener: why not give control order clients and, in view of our overcrowded prisons, convicted criminals as well, an untaxed car? Immediately, we will know the exact location of suspects and crims, solve the prison-overcrowding dilemma (they can sleep in the cars and go out and find a job during the day). A lot cheaper than tagging, and fit for purpose, John . . .

And when it comes to wheezes, it's hard to beat old Gord and his Revenue Rascals. Realising that in July smokers have nowhere to go to indulge in the noxious weed and will perforce have to stub out their last gasper, a rich source of tax will no longer go up in smoke, they invent the Smoke Police, who, at considerable expense to the public purse, will trawl the nation's pubs, clubs and public places, issuing fines for smoking. That should make up the tax shortfall.

Cars for criminals

14 February 2007

'There's nothing on the telly!' is the perennial *cri de cœur* of the embattled senior citizen, particularly now that they have the time to watch daytime television.

A crusty old contributor of mine called Zebedee Doodah strikes the remote control right on the button:

Dear Sir,

I have had the misfortune to have been laid low for the last couple of days with a rather nasty dose of the flu, although the memsahib insists it is nothing more than 'a bit of a sniffle' and that she has been out shovelling snow feeling far worse.

However, during the long days boredom has set in, so it was

suggested by a well-meaning relative that I watch a bit of tele-
vision to pass the time.

'*What would be the point,*' *I replied,* '*of sitting watching*
the test card all day,' *but I was assured that television pro-*
grammes were available during the hours of daylight.

I duly followed the advice and watched programmes about
members of the general public in hospital; members of the
general public selling their household possessions at auction;
members of the general public buying things and then selling
them at auction; members of the general public trying to buy
a house in the UK; members of the general public trying to
buy a house abroad; and so on.

Do you ever look fondly back on the image of that little
girl sitting in front of the blackboard holding a clown and
some balloons?

I do.

This man is leaning against an open door . . .

15 February 2007

Another glittering evening which found me conspicuous by
my absence – the live television coverage of the Brit Awards
last night. Not my kind of thing; I watched a rerun of *Poirot*,
brilliantly played, brilliantly staged, with the utter disregard for
expense that characterised ITV in the good old days. Will we
see its like again, with the art-deco mood of the period so
exquisitely recreated? Good luck to Michael Grade but it's a
big ask . . . Did that 'big ask' bring a sneer to your chiselled

lips? I thought so. Another of those aberrations that have crept into the noble language of Shakespeare while we weren't listening properly, by way of sports commentating: "'E's set 's stall out' . . . 'I hit the ball solid' . . . 'That was a bit tasty' . . . "'E'll be disappointed with that' . . . 'We was unlucky' . . . 'It were never a penalty' . . . And don't give me all that guff about 'an ever-changing' language. Adjectives will never be adverbs, verbs will never be nouns.

Oh yes, the Brits – live for the first time. Oh yeah?

From Reg Raggon:

Morning Wilf!

I'm impressed: a 'live' show where they manage to turn the sound down precisely the moment before anyone says a naughty word. Remarkable!

Anyway, the only act I'd heard of was Bob Dylan, and he didn't win anything.

I liked that Amy Wine-Warehouse though. Perhaps next time she could sing Groucho Marx's 'Lydia (the Tattooed Lady)' . . .

Good to see Take That . . . where was Robbie? Has he left them? I wonder what he's up to these days; you hear so little of him in the news media.

You know Wilf, I've been wondering this long time who Russell Brand has me in mind of and it came to me this morning in the shower. Do you remember Kenny Everett's 'Cupid' – you know, flailing legs, big hair, beard . . . I know young Russell regards the TOGmeister as some sort of mentor, so perhaps when you next tutor him you can suggest he tries out the catchphrase 'It's all in the best POSSIBLE taste'!!

Our Reg is not the first to compare Russell Brand with the late lamented Kenny Everett. There's a physical resemblance there, apart from the manic reckless inspired wit. Kenny and I were friends. I was delighted to play the fall guy in many of his television sketches; he would turn up any time I asked for *Blankety Blank* – and bend my microphone. I like Russell too, as a person and an original performer. Just like Kenny . . . Others see another resemblance:

> *Captain my Captain, I caught the last five minutes of the Bots last night. It's the first time I've seen Russell Brand (I lead a sheltered life). Is it me??? According to surveys he is the man women most want to . . . well, take home as it were. In which home for the bewildered were these surveys carried out? Strikes me he's the long-lost love child of Ken Dodd.*

16 February 2007

The orange light began to flash. Never mind, it's happened before in the middle of my programme, and it's never gone to red alert, panic, get out of there, in the past. Relax, men, it's another false alarm – keep talking, let the music play . . . Then it goes to red! Oh, for heaven's sake! Do we *really* have to leave, abandon the studio, avoid the lifts and walk down the eight flights of stairs? Look, we all know somebody's lit up a surreptitious fag in the gents loo, and for this everybody's rushing around like blue-arsed flies. Oh, all right, I stick on the endless music track, and we're out of there, Barrowlands Boyd and myself, making our leisurely way downstairs devoid of all instincts of self-preservation. I suppose it's the habit, the train-ing, of a job that requires calm in the face of the fumbles, mis-takes and disasters of live broadcasting. It just leaves you ill-equipped for the appropriate panic and urge to flee when something really does go wrong. Remaining calm is fine, but blind panic might just save your life.

So, we gathered on the pavement outside BBC Western House, London W1. Engineers, executives, secretaries, atten-dants, cleaners, technicians, all of 6 Music and Radio 2. Phil Jupitus was wearing a pork-pie hat, which I think he sleeps in. Lesley Douglas, Controller of Radio 2 and 6 Music, British popular radio's equivalent to Catherine the Great, is ill at ease. Listeners may be abandoning her networks in droves and for what? Her question is answered by the arrival of the fire

Fire alarm

brigade, who, in two minutes flat, ascertain that the panic alarm is all due to some sweaty gobdaw taking an excessively steamy shower in the gym in the basement.

Back to the studio – much too late to curb the worst excesses of the listeners:

Don't do that again – consoling music, no Terry – I thought you'd died and was just waiting for 'Water Melon Wine' to be played to confirm my worst fears. Tissues at the ready . . . and blow me you come back. Thank heavens and lots of thanks (to all your witty listeners) for all the laughs! Love Angela x

That was a pleasant break. Will it become a feature of your show?
That's not bad, getting paid to go off and do your exercises.
Bring back 'Fight the Flab' I say. It's a pity that we both seem to have surrendered.

B. KEEPER
NEW FOREST

When the orange light is flashing bright
Things in the gym are not quite right
When it turns to brightest red
Things have got hot at the shower head
So the Togmeister had it on his toes
With six flights of stairs adding to his woes
But as if that wasn't quite enough
Six flights back without losing puff
And all the time making it appear
You didn't spill a drop of bohea.

THE CROOKED MAN OF
OLD BANGOR TOWN

Dear Jerry,
    Enjoyed this morning's radio adaptation of The Towering
Inferno, *wonderfully improvised.*
    Yours,

SIR TIFF HYDE

That's the second time in a couple of months that they've had their hopes dashed over my last goodbye. Am I alone in feeling a sense of anti-climax? I mean, there's the honest listener, ready with the black crêpe, the lilies and the mass cards, not once, but twice – and I'm still here. 'He's taking longer to go than Frank Sinatra. Don't tell me he's going to do farewell concerts, that'd be the last straw . . .'

22 February 2007

The annual TOGs lunch, organised by the mercurial, indefatigable and extremely shy Hellen Bach, with assistance from the loyal and slightly less shy Norm. The Langham Hotel, across the way from Broadcasting House, is the location, as it was last year, thanks to the hotel's kindness and generous discount. The gang's all here, the hard core, the people who write to me every day, whether I read their letters or not. I don't know a single one of them by their real name, but they've become real, true friends – Edina Cloud, Mick Sturbs, Hugh Again, Saunders of Bungay, Don E. Gal – don't start me off, we'll be here all day. They've paid for the doubtful privilege of dining with the likes of me, Deadly, John and Janet Marsh, Fran Godfrey and Beryl Ann Boyd. After a few drinks, we repair to the dining room.

Naturally, I am applauded into the room, but then Deadly enters, to even louder applause. I rise to my feet, exit and enter again to greater applause, rather than be upstaged by a news-reading upstart. John and Janet Marsh then walk in to the loudest applause of the afternoon. There's nothing for it; I rise again, exit and re-enter. I will not be thwarted by these ragamuffins. It might have gone on like that for hours, if the waiters hadn't closed the doors . . .TOGs at play – grown men and women who never lost their sense of fun, their joy of living, people who make me smile and laugh out loud every day of my life. Who still give unsparingly of their time and effort to support *Children in Need* to the tune, so far this year, of almost one and three-quarter million pounds. What have I done to deserve them?

25 February 2007

The Millennium Stadium, Cardiff, for the Carling Cup Final between Arsenal and Chelsea, though I'd rather have been 'off to Dublin in the green' for yesterday's historic rugby union game at Croke Park, Dublin, won, fittingly in the rain, by an Irish side that finally delivered on its promise, obliterating England by a crushing, indeed historic, margin – 43–13 points. I watched the second half in a Welsh hotel room, but my euphoria was quickly dispelled by some of the worst food I've eaten in years. The revival in British cooking still hasn't reached parts of Wales. Years ago, a friend described Cardiff as 'a gastronomic sewer'. There's a hotel over the Severn Bridge still proudly flying the flag . . .

The Millennium Stadium is magnificent, and I stand on the

hallowed turf before the game, watching my friend Lord (Brian) Mawhinney give his usual flawless performance in an interview with Sky Television. A moment later, as I'm admiring him from a distance, I'm told in no uncertain terms by a groundsman to 'get off the pitch'. The fact that I am standing nowhere near the actual playing surface is immaterial; this is the little Hitler's day, and he's making sure everyone knows it. Later, Brian tells me that groundsmen are the uncrowned kings of football, whom owners and managers cross at their peril.

Brian Mawhinney is the reason I'm in Cardiff, and I wouldn't have passed up on Dublin for anyone else. Since he has taken over as chairman of the Football League, he has been a sterling supporter of *Children in Need*, regularly offering a splendid Cup Final-day package to the highest bidder on my Radio 2 'Auction for Things That Money Can't Buy'. This year, Brian and the League have excelled themselves, adding £1 to every ticket sold for today's game. Just before the match, he presents me with a cheque for £70,000. Certainly worth giving up Croke Park for.

It's the first live football game that Helen has ever been to, and I've never seen her more enthralled by the skill and speed of the players. It's certainly the best opening twenty minutes of a football match I've seen, particularly the passing and fluid athleticism of Arsenal's youngsters. Although the Gunners take an early lead, the experience of Chelsea and the lethal striking of Drogba won through in the end, 2–1. The game is marred at the very end by an unseemly punch-up that results in three red cards and two yellow ones, with the referee and both managers, Mourinho and Wenger, struggling to restore order. For a few moments, it's a minor riot and fully displays football's Achilles heel: lack of player discipline. Last evening, I watched a rugby game in which the physical contact was brutal and continuous. At one point, the English lock, Grewcock, went an assault too far. The referee held up a yellow card, Grewcock said, 'Sorry, ref,' and left the field immediately and without complaint from any of his team members. What sort of an example do the petty, girly protests we see every week on Britain's football pitches give to the young?

After the match, we sit in the underground car park of the stadium for an hour, while the crowd disperses. Not that it makes tuppence worth of difference when we eventually take to Cardiff's narrow streets and the inadequate road system. Chepstow's twenty miles away, and it takes us two and a half hours of stop/start crawling. I can't believe that it's like this every time there's a big game at the Millennium and that people are prepared to endure it, however important the occasion. Never again, as far as I'm concerned . . . And what's the traffic going to be like around Wembley, if it's ever built? It was appalling in the old days, and the new stadium will have the capacity for an extra 20,000. Have extra roads been constructed, carriageways widened, car parks extended to cope with thousands more cars? Ask me another. That'll be more great sporting occasions we'll be watching on television, then.

26 February 2007

Twenty-four hours after the most horrific traffic jam of my young life, I'm watching an even worse one from the air, as Helen and I fly into Dubai for a week of rest and recuperation in the desert resort of Al-Maha. We've been there before, and welcomed the peace and solitude of life under canvas on the shifting, whispering, endless sands. That, and the perfect service and excellent food, of course. At ground level, the traffic jam into Dubai (thank Allah, we're going in the opposite direction) knocks the M25 on a Friday evening, or Cardiff on a match day, into a cocked hat. The driver tells me it's the same every evening, from six o'clock to eleven. Some lorry drivers have spent most of their lives in this jam. It's a tribute to man's indomitable spirit, or stupidity, or something. I blame global warming.

27 February 2007

News of the Oscars comes late to Dubai and the sands of the desert, but I see that Al Gore has won one for his documentary rant on climate change. Sorry, but I'm always suspicious of politicians and their motives. Gore's a political has-been who has found a soapbox that has restored his fortunes. Lucky loser. Helen Mirren wins Best Actress for *The Queen,* a racing certainty. She makes an elegant, brief speech. Forest Whitaker, who wins his Oscar for *The Last King of Scotland,* makes a ridiculous, wandering one, in which he implies he may be coming back in the next life to win another Oscar. Jennifer Hudson wins Best Supporting Actress for shrieking through *Dreamgirls* and invokes God, who, apparently, has singled her out for special favour. Martin Scorsese finally gets his Oscar for Best Director for *The Departed,* by no means his best work, and a film almost fatally flawed by Jack Nicholson giving a 'Long John Silver'-type performance that would have embarrassed Robert Newton. Alan Arkin wins the award for Best Supporting Actor for *Little Miss Sunshine*, but he couldn't hold a candle to Leslie Phillips in *Venus*. The frocks are everywhere, but who invited Posh? There she is, waif-like, still striking that silly, sulky Spice Girl pose. For heaven's sake, somebody give her something to do while she's in LA. Revive the Spice Girls! Take That came back from the dead, didn't they?

1 March 2007

Another day in paradise: a camel train wends its way across the desert, the rare oryx crops the few blades of grass beside our tent, unafraid, the little birds sing in the hedges, a gentle zephyr stirs the timeless sands as the sun beats down. I'm expecting Omar Sharif to come riding his camel out of the haze at any moment . . . The *Gulf News*, glossy, in full colour, is delivered every morning and would put any British newspaper to shame. A mixture of tabloid and broadsheet, it covers the world as well as the United Arab Emirates, and in its editorials and features is a breath of liberal fresh air in a Muslim world that appears to us in the West to have been taken over by rabid fundamentalists. Every day the paper carries at least two colour photos of Dubai's ruler, always giving his full name and title: His Highness Shaikh Mohammed bin Rashid al Maktoum, Vice-President and Prime Minister of the UAE and Ruler of Dubai. Today there are three photos.

Prince Charles and the Duchess of Cornwall are visiting the Emirates. Yesterday they were here in Dubai, and my heart goes out to him, trekking around in eighty-plus degrees, in suit, collar and tie, expected to look interested in everything from basket-weaving to drains. No wonder his princely reserve cracks – he's just made another gaffe, one of those whispered asides that seem to reverberate around the world: 'Get rid of McDonald's.' Bound to make the headlines in Britain, where the current obsession of the media is with obese children and their unfortunate parents, who, as usual, are getting all the blame. Never mind – next week it will be some other bandwagon, and it will be as if fat kids never existed.

Refreshing to see Al Gore, a man I trust about as far as I could throw Bill Clinton, exposed as a blatant abuser in his private life of the carbon footprint that he so excoriates in public. They're lying in wait for you, Al, they even got Caesar's wife in the end . . .

6 March 2007

I'm in south-west France, making sure that the house hasn't fallen down and paying the bills. It's a far cry from the desert of Dubai as the rain drips from the eaves, but all is tranquil, and there's always the television . . . In common with every British ex-pat and property owner in Europe 'neath the satellite footprint, we enjoy the same television output as in faraway Blighty. I'm sure it's why many Brits continue to flee their native shores. It can't just be the better weather, or the cheaper cost of living, or Gordon Brown. Watching *Sky News* trying to keep up with the 'cash for honours' scandal that has been dogging Tony Blair's footsteps for over a year and is the last thing he needs on top of his travails over Iraq, Afghanistan, global warming and Gordon Brown (talk about an *éminence grise*!). Kay Burley, sharp, pert, head cocked to one side as always, calls in a reporter from outside rain-dashed Number 10: 'Hello to you,' she greets him, brightly. Two more reports later, and she's done the 'Hello to you' trick twice more, and I'm shouting at her. What the hello happened to good old 'Hello'? Where does 'to you' come in? Who else is the woman talking to? It might be permissible if she's greeting not only the reporter but passers-by: 'Hello to you, and that woman in the red hat.' I detected this irritating, pointless over-elaboration first among BBC weather forecasters: 'Good evening to you – let's put some detail on this map here . . .', but somehow you expect this kind of foolishness from weather forecasters, whose span upon the stage is brief, and who need to make it count.

It's not just the 'Hello to you' that brings out the hidden curmudgeon, it's the 'Thank you very much indeed's and the 'Many thanks indeed's with which every reporter and weatherman is fulsomely rewarded every morning on the *Today* programme on Radio 4. For heaven's sake, reporting and forecasting is their job, why the effusive thanks? Useless to complain; the smarmy habit has spread all over television news like a rash. It can only be a matter of time before the elongated 'thank you's are followed by further effusions: 'That was an excellent report/weather forecast, you're in particularly good form today, and looking so well, that colour suits you . . .' Can we get on with the news, please? Thank you so much . . . Which reminds me of a news 'anchor' – that's what they call 'em in the States – whom I heard reward a contributor with 'Thank you much!' Not 'very much' – just 'much'. He did it several times, so it must be his thing, his signature. I can imagine him, at the beginning of his career, racking his brains on how to be a 'different' anchor, how to attract attention, how to stand out in a boatload of anchors. Then, a light bulb goes on over his head 'Thank you much!' Nobody else says that, nobody has even thought of it! Major network news, here I come! And he did . . .

American television – what can you make of it? On the one hand, it produces an endless stream of brilliant sit-coms and series, superbly scripted and acted, at a time when British television, for all its excellence, can only replicate once in a blue moon. *Frasier, Friends, ER, Boston Legal, Seinfeld, Cheers,* many more, that go to make up a long list of wonderful, entertaining television. You think it must reflect the sharp intelligence of the average American viewer – until you watch their talk shows. Are these made for a different kind of American? A sub-human stratum that only watches late at night? If you've missed the delights of Leno, Letterman and O'Brien, lucky you. A nightly show of talk, comedy and music is the toughest gig on television, and it has long since drained Leno and Letterman of whatever charm and wit they first possessed. Their shrieking, mindless audiences alone are enough to have reduced them to the mere ciphers that they are now. But it's Conan O'Brien that really makes you question the sanity of the American viewer, or indeed the network that allows him air time. This is a tall, thin, frenetic, overexcited schoolboy in his mid-forties, with no idea how to deliver a punchline, who shouts, screams and is completely ill at ease, from the moment he comes on stage looking like somebody has just plugged him into the mains to the moment he leaves to have his batteries recharged for the following night. It's sheer embarrassment from beginning to end, and it makes me feel that I must be missing something or, more worryingly, that we and the Americans are separated by more than just a common language.

8 March 2007

Tony Blair says that he would like to get involved more closely with environmental issues when his time is up at Number 10. Climate change, the last refuge of the failed politician. Perhaps Mr Blair is seeking to emulate the opportunistic Al Gore, who has revived his fortune on the back of global warming. Tony could link up with Sir Jonathon Porritt, who, in fairness, has been banging on about this class of thing for hundreds of years, mainly in Prince Charles's ear.

Everybody pays lip-service to the idea of combating climate change, but nobody really gives a toss – Al Gore's carbon footprint is bigger than anybody else's in his area, and I'll take a small bet that Prince Charles's one is bigger than most in Wiltshire. And now we learn that the very government departments that are so insistent that we curtail our carbon emissions, our water consumption, and generally behave responsibly to the planet, are themselves wasting more water and extending their carbon emissions, in some cases by forty per cent!

Nuclear power is the obvious answer to conserving our resources, but a green-whipped government insists on desecrating our coastlines with thousands of useless windmills that will never supply the electrical power needed.

It's no wonder people get testy:

This weekend's dinner party was a cracker. We were all reducing our carbon footprints by turning off the streetlights. Brilliant. This is the kind of wheeze dreamed up by people who:

1. *Never go out*
2. *Do not have a river between them and the pub*
3. *Are not bothered by footpads.*

The rest of us will continue to behave normally and ignore all this hoo-ha until someone starts being serious about it all.

   I offer the following as evidence that we are getting serious:

1. *No ice in any drinks – to save power*
2. *No importing of mineral water – to save transport costs and to spite the French*
3. *Kids walking to school.*
Yeah right. Wake me when any of the above happens.

SAUNDERS OF BUNGAY

Al Gore

13 March 2007

I've been presenting the Oldie of the Year Awards for what must seem like a lifetime, to the great and the good who turn up every year at Simpsons in the Strand for a school dinner and an afternoon of the wry eccentricity that characterises Richard Ingrams's wonderful monthly magazine, a beacon for the senior citizen who still has 'snap in his celery'. Every passing year seems to bring a more dazzling turnout, a shining tribute to the esteem and affection in which Ingrams is held by his peers. I've seen the late Dennis Thatcher, Bill Deedes, Peregrine Worsthorne, seated together at the top table, all fast asleep ... This year's line-up of guests would flatter the BAFTAs: Peter O'Toole, Leslie Phillips, Tom Courtenay, Sinead Cusack, Jeremy Irons, Tom Conti. Then there's Clare Short MP, Peter Alliss, Melvyn Bragg, John Mortimer – and they're only the ones who catch my eye, as I rise to address the distinguished gathering. They're a wonderful audience, too well mannered, too well stricken in years perhaps, to recall the old gags I've been recycling for years. Even Barry Cryer pretends to laugh ... I explain to the audience the exacting, rigorous process by which I, as chairman, and a panel of experts consisting of Ned Sherrin, Maureen Lipman, Jon Snow, Gyles Brandreth and Editor Ingrams select the winners of the awards. The cut and thrust of argument, point and counterpoint, heated disagreement, as finally, exhausted, we reach our decisions. The judges leave, satisfied with a job well done and then, as ever, Richard Ingrams returns to his eyrie and decides who's really going to win. It's a process as old as time and the *Oldie* itself. The winners rise to universal acclaim, each of them

It's the rare unsigned ones you want . . . September 2006. (Jonathan Hordle/Rex Features)

A Service of Celebration
for the Life and work of
PAUL CHRISTOPHER WALTERS
(PAULY)
1947 – 2006

The Parish Church of St Peter and St Paul,
Kimpton
November 2nd 2006

Right

Holding my Lifetime Achievement Award in Limerick, February 2007. Bertie Ahern had just been elected Taoiseach again, despite this photograph . . . (Michael Cowhey, *Business Limerick* magazine)

Below

It might have been worse – we could have come last . . . Eurovision 2007 hopefuls Scooch. (©BBC)

Above
Any sign of the ball?

Right
A lifetime ambition fulfilled: I can drive a herd of sheep up O'Connell Street, Limerick, whenever I like. Receiving the freedom of the city in June 2007.

Top to bottom

Adorable, these little creatures of the wild, the lesser bearded Oddie and the curly Katie . . . On the *Springwatch* set in June, with Julie and Stephen Stannard, generous donators to *Children in Need.*

I owe it all to endless rehearsal and steady drinking . . .

Top
David Hatch as I'll always remember him – with Roger Royle, at Alan and Kate's wedding.

Above
Laughingly called 'the Team'. Me, me and me and underlings, from left: Taffy Traffic Totty, Chazzanova, Beryl Ann Boyd, Wealdstone Wonderboy, Boggy Stud-Muffin, Posh Bink.

rewarded with a trophy, a shining example of the Taiwanese plastic-mouldmaker's art.

The cream of Britain's press always turn up, so I'm awaiting the cross-questioning on something that exercised tabloids and broadsheets alike while I was away on holiday. The Freedom of Information Act threw up the fact that the BBC has been paying me to present *Children in Need* on live television's big night. It was enough to create a frenzy: 'Scandalous!' 'How can he, it's a charity!' and much more offensive tosh that I was lucky enough to miss. I knew that it was going on, of course, but decided, based on previous long experience of the press and its ways, that the old axiom of 'don't complain, don't explain' and simply starve the wicked story of the oxygen of publicity, was the only sensible alternative. The BBC issued a statement pointing out that I had never asked for, never negotiated, a payment, but that they paid me a nominal amount every year, just as they paid everyone else taking part in the show: producer, director, cameramen, soundmen, musicians, floor managers and the hundreds of others that make the seven-hour live television spectacular such a success. They pointed out that it was they, the BBC, that paid me, not the charity. Of course, the facts didn't get as much coverage as the 'scandal', but then they never do. And there will always be people waiting to believe only the worst, so what's the point in my saying that I've never taken a penny from any of the hundreds of charities I've helped over the years, that I've been with *Children in Need* since the very beginning, and between us, the British public and I have raised almost £400 million for the charity, and every penny of that has gone to the children. Last year, I raised almost half a million pounds in four mornings on my radio show in the 'Auction for Things That Money Can't Buy'. I got paid to do that radio show. It's what I do, and the BBC pays me to do it. Not *Children in Need* for heaven's sake! One is a broadcaster, the other is a charity! But why am I shouting at you? It's just the disappointment, I suppose, that after all these years anybody would even think that I would take a penny from *Children in Need.*

15 March 2007

Further proof, if proof were needed, that they're not all locked up yet: in view of the scandalous overcrowding in prisons, and the impossibility of cramming in any more wrongdoers in police cells, it's just been suggested that supermarkets and shopping malls should be allowed to incarcerate suspected shoplifters, muggers and general thugs in holding cells for up to four hours, until innocence or guilt is proven. The listener pointed out that there's nothing new in the world; this method was used in every village in the country in the dim and distant past. It was called 'the stocks'.

Then a TOG named Eric Rundle summed it up, as only a crusty Old Geezer can:

> *Dear Tel*
> *At last all is clear. For the last 25 years, unknown to the customers, my local supermarket has been a test bed for the four-hour holding cell.*
> *They referred to it as the Express Checkout.*
> *Yours aye . . .*

16 March 2007

Masterchef Goes Large has been keeping my listeners amused and annoyed in roughly equal parts. It should have been entitled 'Masterchef Goes Loud'. The two presenters – Greg, the 'ingredients expert' and John, the 'internationally famous chef' – have worn the viewers' patience thin with their bellowing – 'It doesn't get tougher than this!', 'A good plate of food!' – and their stuffing of forkfuls of the contestants' best efforts into their capacious maws.

My favourite curmudgeon, Stewart Eglin of Kirkcaldy, was leaning against an open door as far as I was concerned, with this letter, following last night's grand finale:

> *So there we have it then. We have a new Masterchef – and I have to confess that I am completely baffled. How was he chosen? During the week we have had the contestants cook for schoolchildren, for the army, for Michelin-starred chefs and for two prime ministers. They went off on a jolly to do a bit of cooking in Paris. Despite all of that, the decision appears to have been based on the final meal delivered to John Torode and the shouting greengrocer. Why???*
>
> *I'm sure the winner is a delightful chap. He certainly has a 'signature' walk, as they say in cooking circles – he was able to roll, waddle and mince all at the same time.*

TOGs take no prisoners, but I'm bound to say that all along I've been bewailing the futility of cooking for squaddies, schoolchildren and the rest, and whole segments of the show being given over to the hopeful cooks helping out in classy restaurants. Just an exercise in eking out a good idea to fill the schedules. Everybody knows that the only test that was going to count was the final cook-out, and so it proved. A little chap called Steven won.

So it's all over for another year at *Masterchef*. I was glad that Steven won; after all what use is a 'trends analyst' that still thinks designer stubble is in? Good luck to him as chef is all I say.

We gave so much publicity to *Masterchef* that the production team sent me a basket of cakes. I notice I didn't get any fresh vegetables. Steven, the winner, and Hannah, one of the runners-up, have offered to cook for me. Watch this diary . . .

17 March 2007

Every so often, a hint of *Finnegans Wake* or Myles na gCopaleen wafts, wraithlike, into the radio show, and always provokes a response of streams of semi-consciousness. The other day I mentioned that I had met Brendan Behan once, in a Dublin pub. Nothing remarkable about it: everybody who ever took a drink in a Dublin pub met Brendan Behan at least once. A lovely letter from Barrington (RN Ret'd) had a tale of the late, great Brendan, who, when asked by a literary lady to define the difference between poetry and prose in his work, replied:

> *There was a young man called McFee,*
> *Who worked for Accles and Pollocks,*
> *He went for a walk by the sea*
> *And the water came up to his knees.*

'That's prose, Missus,' says Brendan, 'but another few inches of water, and it would have been poetry.'

I am sick of telling people that in my youth the only people who celebrated St Patrick's Day with a parade were expatriates in Boston, Chicago and New York. The idea of anyone dyeing the Liffey or the Shannon green, or even dyeing the sacred pint of stout a similar colour, while policemen marched up O'Connell Street behind pipe bands, would have been regarded as dangerous lunacy. 'Hail glorious Saint Patrick', fair enough, for giving us a day off in the middle of Lent when we could eat and drink what we liked, as long as we went to Mass and wore a sprig of shamrock in our buttonholes.

So it was with no sense of disappointment that I presented myself in Maidstone, Kent TV's, studios this afternoon to cajole the suffering masses into voting for the song to represent the UK in this year's Eurovision Song Contest, to be held in Helsinki in May. Finland's the place because last year, in Athens, a group of surpassingly ugly Goths called Lordi shrieked their way to victory with their own particular vision of hell on wheels. They sung tonight as well, to show it was no fluke, featuring half-naked women in cages and fireworks going off in all directions. It was recorded, but they did it in one take, a tribute possibly to their professionalism, or possibly because it's the only song in their repertoire.

Anyway, at half-seven, the pretty and excellent Fearne Cotton and I trooped out to introduce the six songs that had fought their way into consideration for the supreme honour of representing the UK in Helsinki. A motley collection, as ever, so we tried to enliven it with comments from Mel Giedroyc and John Barrowman, and votes from forty-one foreigners, representing all the countries in this year's contest. Mel and John were jolly, but the opinions of the forty-one were vital, since we can't vote for ourselves and their fellow-nationals would be the ones to pass judgement on the UK representative's efforts. Johnny Foreigner picked a black 'bling' act called Big Brovaz and a French balladeer named Cyndi. Needless to say, this inside information was ignored by the great British public, who voted a camp airline cabin-crew send-up by Scooch, the winner.

By the time you read this, the Eurovision Song Contest will be a hazy memory, but if Scooch win for the UK, you can have this book for nothing . . .

However, the big story was *me*. The buck stopped elsewhere, but I'll be taking the rap in tomorrow's papers for announcing Cyndi as the winner. Once again, there's no point in the explaining or complaining. It was live television, it happened, it was over in a flash, and, thank heaven, nobody died.

19 March 2007

The press had a field day. Following the *Children in Need* rubbish, it was open season on our hero. 'Woeful Wogan gets his comeuppance' was one of the kinder headlines. A fellow in *The Times* said that I would carry the gaffe to my grave. A pretty sweeping statement, when you consider a career studded with pratfalls. My public, as ever, reacted without even a suggestion of sympathy for a doddering presenter with both feet in his mouth:

May I congratulate you on the exciting and innovative way you announced the final result on 'Making Mistakes Up' on Saturday.

I wonder if your other listener has realised that this is a technique you 'borrowed' from your weather numpties who for years have been entertainingly fooling us with their forecasts.

Yours etc.

JAMIE DOUGHNUT

Congratulations, Sir Terry, on creating such a thrilling climax to Making Your Mind Up *on Saturday night. Would it be the Loch Lomond remix by Cyndi, who could at least sing in tune, or Pooch, the budget air stewards and esses, who pretended to fly like planes like my toddlers do?*

Lots of meaningful pauses or tog-induced why am I here? lapses of memory later and you told us . . . and we still didn't know . . . excellente herr togmeister. Keep up the good work. There will always be room here for you at Haveyouseenmy Keys Home for the Perpetually Confused, Florida.

The Ukrainian drag queen entry will be quaking in her size 16 tackety boots.

Yours

CARRIE R PIGEON

You'll have seen it by now, but the UK entry has been drawn very late in the game, following the aforementioned Ukrainian transvestite.

Now you may come in for some gentle ribbing over the Cyndi v Scooch business over the next few days so here's my advice to put a positive spin on it.

Just look 'em in the eye and say that you were putting down a marker for next year's Brits show and that you and Fearne quite fancy the gig as the new Mick and Sam.

Failing that, just tell them that it was quite impossible to concentrate on the job in hand, what with all the racket and young Fearne Cotton's dress being on back to front.

ALASTAIR CAMPBELL

I don't think that's the *real* Alastair Campbell, but you never know.

I know this, though. It'll take a week for my listeners to get over this chance to knock seven bells out of me. Bless 'em . . .

20 March 2007

It's the little things that catch the eye and take the fancy, although perhaps the opening of the Sky Walk over the Grand Canyon is not such a little thing. This is a semi-circular stroll, but at the cost of several million dollars, which enables you to amble over the edge of the Canyon and look down into the depths without falling several miles down to your eternal reward. The BBC sent a reporter to cover the grand opening, but it proved something of an anti-climax. My reaction to the report was exactly the same as that of my correspondent Cliff Hanger:

I watched the BBC news in great anticipation last night to see the opening of the Sky Walk over the Grand Canyon. How disappointed I was to realise that Auntie had sent a cameraman who was afraid of heights to cover the event. He never went anywhere near the edge. While being told 'looking through the glass floor, made up of five layers, three inches thick, you can see 4,000 feet down', what could we see? A lump of rock barely 10 feet below! Poor chap, I do sympathise as I am scared of heights too, but wasn't there someone else who could hold the camera?

I must say that I thought cameraman and reporter both lacking in pluck and the proper newshound spirit. I'm no one to talk – when the present Lady Wogan and I visited that great wonder of the world, we were entranced by the view and the ever-changing colours of the Canyon, without ever putting a foot closer than ten yards from the edge.

25 March 2007

The Archbishop of Canterbury, a decent man who has done his bit before now on my daily God-spot, 'Pause for Thought', has come out strongly in favour of a British apology, and possible reparations, for the country's role in the slave trade a couple of hundred years ago. Not everybody agrees with him, but my TOGs have their own way of putting it:

Mrs Nobby Clark, my wife, had just finished two hours of ironing, I said to her when you have cleaned the car done the washing up done the vaccing and made the dinner we could sit down and watch that programme about William Wilberforce, who abolished slavery. I said haven't we moved on . . . She hasn't answered yet. Why has she poured custard in my shoes????

As it looks like the country is going to go down on bended knee to apologise for slavery, I think it's time I came clean too.

According to one of my relatives, who has one of those 'find your ancestors' PC programmes, and way too much time on his hands, it appears that the Sinfields arrived with Johnny Foreigner at the Battle of Hastings.

We didn't do much in the way of fighting, we just went to Luton and worked in the hat factory, but nevertheless, I would sincerely like to apologise to King Harold for the thing with the eye.

There, I feel better for that, we are now healed as a nation.

ROB SINFIELD,
SAILSWORTH, GLOS.

Honestly, if we are to start apologising for everything that happened in our history, where will it all end? For example, are you going to demand that Tony Blair apologises for pinching the Wogan Estates from Wales, and demand reparations from Golden Brown for many centuries of loss of income from them?

That was from Heidi Vodka – I know it was only a matter of time before it got personal. It's my own fault: I have, from time to time, whined on a bit about the English taking the Wogan castles in Wales, causing some of us to cross the Irish Sea, where we built more castles, only for the English to take them away from us again. I'm not bitter, but where will the apologising end? To Ireland, for the Great Famine, to the Scots for the Clearances, to India and Africa for exploitation? To *Children in Need*, for taking VAT from the *Janet and John* CDs? Up off your knees; and don't do it again.

Sorry

27 March 2007

Drained of all emotion from apologising we must still keep our wits about us, if we're not all to go up in smoke – the herds of wildebeest which Basil Fawlty imagined he could see from his hotel bedroom window could well be a reality by next Thursday, if the more excitable of the doom-mongers are to be believed. In the meantime, we must keep our eyes peeled for a horse midge, which, attracted by the searing heat, might come over here from Africa. This dreadful creature causes sickness and death not only in African horses, but also in mules, donkeys and zebras. Unless we change our light bulbs, use less toilet paper, and pay more taxes for driving and flying, our four-legged friends could be in trouble. Still, every cloud . . . Thanks, he's sure, to global warming, a listener's lawnmower started after only three pulls, having been left in the garden shed for the whole winter.

We're just coming up to the time of year that defines mankind: the grass-cutting, lawnmowing season. For we are not divided by North and South, nor even by Man U and non-Man U. The great divide is between those who enjoy cutting the grass and those who think it the most monumental waste of time ever invented by some ancient Titchmarsh. No prizes for guessing into which camp I lazily tumble. Apart from the mind-numbing tedium of marching up and down, trying to keep your lines straight with fumes getting up your nose and daisies, dandelions and earthworms flying in all directions, trying to start the damned mower is enough to test the patience of a saint. You put it away in the late autumn, serviced, oiled, cleaned, under its nice warm sheet, ready for the challenge of the spring, knowing in your heart that you're whistling Dixie. It's not going to start.

In my experience, small-boat engines are exactly the same. Out of the water for the winter, polished, primped, prepared, cosseted and wrapped in swaddling clothes; into the water for the summer, zip, *nada* – where's the mechanic? I've had a couple of small boats, one in a marina in Spain and the other on the Thames, and it's true what they say: the two happiest days of your life are when you buy a boat and when you sell it. Mind you, I should have had enough self-knowledge not to bother. Anything mechanical, anything inanimate, anything at all that takes time or trouble has no place in my life. I don't like brushing my teeth, taking a shower, tying shoelaces, shaving. I hated skiing because of the boots. I have no capacity for 'taking pains'. I'd never have made a producer, a director or an editor. That's why I thank whatever God made me for the job I'm in.

I'm forever being asked, 'What time do you get in to your studio?', 'How long do you rehearse?', 'Do you prepare the night before?', 'Do you do a lot of research?', 'Who writes the script?', 'Do your staff have it all ready for you when you come in in the morning?', 'What do you do when the show is over?' Look, I leave my house at 6.15 in the morning, greet my producer, Barrowlands Boyd (or Beryl Ann Boyd, depending on his mood), who's having a reflective gasper outside BBC Western House, at five past seven. We exchange civilities with Judy and Smokey, the two receptionists, and make our way in the lift that claims it can carry six people, but is a tight squeeze for Boyd and myself, well covered as we are. We pause to shoot the breeze on the sixth floor with Traffic Totty, the Tart from Penarth, Lynn Bowles, wave cordially to the dozing newsreader in his little cell, and then it's heads down into the cauldron that is Studio 6C. We wake the technical operator, I switch on the computers, test the microphone and the various circuits and thingymebobs, Boydy throws the 500 or so emails that have festered overnight at me, and, Sarah Kennedy permitting, it's 7.30, the newsmonger does a couple of minutes, and it's my turn. With any luck, it's National Bacon Butty / Sausage / Curry / Cheese / Pie / Sandwich Week, so there may be provender to stay our echoing tums. If not, we must wait until 8.20, when the insanely lovely Peta rushes bacon or sausage butties to our starving sides from the canteen. She crosses several roads to deliver these vittles from the BBC canteen, which is shrewdly placed half a mile away, down Regent Street. Drawn by the scent, people drop by – new-shawkers, travel trollops, hungry producers from less fortunate shows, Ken Bruce, Dame Lesley Douglas, finest controller of programmes in the history of radio. Two hours drift idly by and, almost as soon as I have arrived, it's time to fold our tents and silently steal away. That's it – no preparation, no fraught discussions before or after the programme, no script, no research, just a technical operator, a producer and me. Oh, and Eileen O'Rourke, secretary to toffs and gentry. With eight mil-lion listeners, we must be the most cost-effective programme in the history of broadcasting.

29 March 2007

First *Points of View* of the bright new year, hurrah! Not that the BBC think much of it, moving it around from Billy to Jack on a Sunday evening, like the filler they obviously think it is. We're lucky to get fifteen minutes of transmission time, which you might think shows scant regard for what the licence-fee payers think of the BBC's output, but I couldn't possibly com-ment. You may also think it strange that *Points of View* is not transmitted during the peak viewing seasons of autumn and winter, but again . . . You might also go so far as to wonder why, given the enormous weekly output of four television channels, only fifteen minutes a week is devoted to viewers' comments, but then . . .

Points of View, whether anybody really cares, is a pleasure to present. I've been lucky to have a series of wonderful, efficient, professional producers over the years, the kind of people who know what they want, and do it quickly, without doing it all twice in case you got it wrong the first time. My kind of people.

They've all been women since I started the show six or more years ago and, if they try to slip a male producer across me, I'm outta there. I've got two Carolines as I write – Caroline Jones from BBC Birmingham and the exec from Manchester, Caroline Roberts. It's not entirely a female coven; there's master lighting cameraman Pete and super soundmen, Geraint or John. With make-up and autocue, that's six people producing fifteen minutes of mainstream television. The second most cost-effective programme in the history of broadcasting. The show is recorded in one of the reception rooms of the UK's grandest, and probably most expensive, hotel, Cliveden, where once the Astors presided in grandeur, and John Profumo, Christine Keeler and the rest came to such spectacular grief. To look out across the terrace to the grand parterre garden, and on to the Thames, as it winds its timeless way, is a weekly treat. And the viewing public think it's my house.

The difference between the radio listeners who write to me every day with their quirky, witty views on whatever they watched the previous night on television, and the viewers who write to *Points*, is like chalk and cheese. Whereas the radio crowd take their viewing with a pinch of salt, *Points'* correspondents take it very seriously indeed, with little or no humour. Currently, my radio people are knocking seven good-humoured bells out of Jennie Bond and her admittedly egregious presence on *The Great British Menu*; *Points of View*ers haven't even noticed dear Jennie and her terrible French. They're saving their spleen for *Castaway*, *Panorama* and 'serious' programmes. Nobody writes to *Points* about *EastEnders*. My radio listeners send up the soap on a daily basis. I don't believe that the two audiences are that radically different. They're both, probably, what's known to demographers as 'Middle England', the people who vote our governments in and out of power. Same sort of people, different outlook. I'm glad I'm not a politician . . .

31 March 2007

Lunch at home, with Janet and John Marsh, Canon Roger Royle, Alan Dedicoat and Alan Boyd. It's an inadequate thank you to 'Boggy' Marsh for his friendship and the practised grumpiness that has so endeared him to listeners of 'Wake Up To Wogan' over the long, weary years. His wheezing, uncontrolled laughter time and again reduced countless listeners to similar paroxyms; thank goodness they are preserved forever on *Janet and John Reloaded*, the double CD that is the follow-up to the first 'Janet and John', which made well over £1 million for *Children in Need* last year and is still selling. With the Treasury's refunding of VAT to the tune of £300,000, I'll be amazed if Part One doesn't make the £2 million mark; and similarly astonished if *Reloaded* hasn't passed the million mark by next November's *Children in Need* big night, although the Treasury did say that last year's refund of tax was a 'one-off' . . . Janet Marsh has borne the burden of being the 'straight man' of 'Janet and John' with queenly fortitude – without her forbearance it could never have happened.

It's a lovely lunch: we drink champagne as we stroll down

the avenue of cherry trees, and all is good-humour and laughter. After all, we're not losing Boggy. He claims to be retiring,
but he'll be back at regular intervals, or whenever the mood
takes him, to reduce all around him to mild hysteria. The good
Canon Royle, who is in a permanent state of hysteria, and
whose snorting laughter has frightened the horses for years,
also makes spurious claims of retirement, having passed on
Radio 2's *Sunday Half-Hour* to Father Brian D'Arcy. Roger will
still contribute to my 'Pause for Thought', thank goodness.
This outstanding man, whose cheery exterior masks a loving
kindness and a generosity of spirit that I have never seen
excelled, has helped my three children to celebrate their marriages in a true spirit of Christianity, with love and laughter.
He has been joined in this by my great friend, Father Brian,
the only person I know to match Roger for sheer goodness,
kindness and, although it will embarrass them both, holiness –
or at least, holiness as I understand it. The two Alans will, I
hope, sustain me and the listeners with their wit and professionalism for years to come. If we're spared, as my redoubtable
friend and colleague, Sarah Kennedy, puts it.

2 April 2007

Girding his loins for the 'scorching' summer that global warming will undoubtedly bring, and all that will entail for the
garden, a listener found himself at his local Homebase in dire
need of nylon pea-and-bean netting and a new trowel.
Presenting himself at the checkout, he was surprised – as a
fifty-eight-year-old with white hair – to be asked to confirm

that he was over eighteen years of
age. Upon enquiring which of his
two purchases (pea-and-bean
netting; trowel) might be
thought to contain alcohol, he
was informed that it was nothing to do with the demon drink, it
was the trowel, which could be used
as an 'offensive weapon'. He left
Homebase with head held high, a

Trowel

man living life on the edge, his trowel at hand (well, in his
inside pocket). Suddenly, dangerous, he's thinking of buying a
special chain to attach his dibber to his belt.

My heart goes out to another listener, this time a worried
one. Not in the first flush of youth, she finds herself out of
work. 'Jobless' being such an unedifying description of her lot,
she wonders if the old thespian euphemism of 'resting' might
be more acceptable. What about 'set aside'? It has a dignified
poignancy, and may well attract an EU grant.

What with 'Elfin Safety', diversity, compliance and keeping
it all green, you need to pick your words with extreme care
these days. A teacher tells me that his school, having lost a fair
proportion of its teachers to retirement, promotion and disil-
lusionment, and one newly qualified teacher having been
made into a meat pie by Year 6, needed to advertise to attract
new staff. The advertisement was sent to Birmingham Local
Authority for approval. The authority lost no time in inform-
ing the school that the words 'dynamic' and 'enthusiastic'
could not be used, as they were 'ageist'. Perhaps the offending
words could be replaced with the more neutral 'lazy old gits
need not apply'.

4 April 2007

French Railway's TGV hits 356 miles per hour (no idea what that is in kilometres) to smash the rail speed record. That's three times faster than the fastest we can muster. Ah, these lost glory days when Britain led the world with the Mallard and the Flying Scotsman. I see a very senior spokesman interviewed this evening on television, who, when asked for his reaction, says, 'Well, France is three times bigger than Britain.' That's the spirit.

Keith Richards, the original shocker, has come up trumps again – and just in time for another Stones tour – by telling the world that he probably snorted his father's ashes along with a line of coke he was shoving up his nose at the time. There's a suspicion among my media-savvy listeners that Keith may be having us on by re-creating a story that appeared in *The Times* some years ago, when burglars broke into a house and, finding a box labelled 'Charlie', took time out to snort the contents. It turned out that Charlie was the homeowner's pet Labrador, which had been cremated the previous week.

It's extraordinary; I still have no idea what gets my listeners' creative juices going. You think you're on to a good thing that will get the pot a-bubbling, and the reaction is zip, *nada*. Then the late great Pauly Walters mentions a tin of rhubarb that he's been keeping for sentimental reasons, and we're going down for a third time in a flood of mail! Yesterday, Taffy Traffic Totty, Lynn Bowles, made casual mention of Clarkes Pies, an impor-tant formative influence in every Welsh person's life, apparently.

The heavens opened, and it rained emails, letters and post-cards. Dai the Pie made the blasphemous claim that the pies weren't even made in Wales!

> As an exiled taff now living in Bristol, the pies made here (Clarkes) are not a patch on the real Welsh McCoy. Ron Evans pies!!! made in Taibach, Port Talbot. They knock any other pie into a cocked hat!! I have them smuggled across the Severn Bridge in hollowed-out sheep, My 'Mam Gi' (Gran) swore by Ron Evans Pies and said that if you had some dreadful disease or other it could be cured by rubbing in a Ron Evans Pie. Has Lynn, the beautiful, exiled, red-haired, Welsh Princess (Y Ddraig Goch) not ever had a Ron Evans Pie . . . she must have had a very sheltered life.

Ron Evans Pies the best? Dai of Bucks knows better:

> Does the traffic Blodwyn know of Monks pies, cooked by Mr Monk the butcher on Crwys Road, Cardiff? – these had more meat than the infamous Clarkes Pie.

Terry Stevens strikes back in the name of Welsh Pride:

> Once again the English are trying to get in on the act and make claim to a Welsh institution. Clarkes Pies were made by two brothers called Dutch. And have been and continue to be made at their two shops in Grangetown and Victoria Park, Cardiff. PS. is Lovely Lyn one of the famous Bowles family who ran a sand/dredging company in Grangetown?

Yes, but she'd no idea things were going to get this personal.

Then they really began to get heated north of a line drawn from Birmingham to the Wash:

Listen 'ere mate, if ye want a good pie thi'sen oop 'ere te Barnsley fer Percy Potter's Pork Pies. Yev niver tasted pies till yev tasted Potters. Nah then!!

ANN FROM SUNNY DONNY

I left it there. I have a memory of eating a pie in Blackpool, where David Vine and I were compèring the Miss United Kingdom Contest, in those far-off days before feminism, political correctness and Germaine Greer.

I made a total cock of things on the night, getting my prompt cards mixed up and not knowing Miss Bristol from Miss Oldham, and I blame that pie. I bit into it with every reason to expect, if not fillet steak, an unidentifiable but chewable piece of meat. I got potatoes. I couldn't believe it – a potato pie? Every one I've eaten ever since has given me indigestion, including a foot-long Cornish pasty that fell from my nerveless fingers and covered the floor of an outside broadcast vehicle to a depth of two feet.

6 April 2007

It's Good Friday, I'm off today for the Easter holiday, and not back to work until Tuesday. My listeners make no secret of their resentment at my few days off and cards wishing me a 'Happy Easter' are remarkable by their absence. As far as my crowd are concerned, Easter, like Christmas, summer, pop music and television, is not what it was. An old Wogan hand, Pauline Lynch of Great Yarmouth, puts it tersely: 'I can remember when Easter meant church, picnics and eating chocolate. Now it means going to buy a cheap leather suite . . . ' As ever on bank holidays, the television commercials are awash with furniture and DIY. I can't think of anything worse than spending even a minute of what should be a time of rest and recreation amid the heaving masses of World of Leather or IKEA. Mind you, it's years since I've been to a supermarket, and I was reminded why the other day at our local post office. I lined up behind an extremely overweight woman who was doing her weekly shop of cigarette papers, tobacco and every possible variation of lottery ticket. She turned to me: 'Are you who I think you are?' 'No, he's a much younger man.' (Statutory reply, usually allows me to exit with a smile.) 'Oh,' she ripostes. 'Well, they always say that television puts on pounds. Not in your case, eh? Ha! Ha!' Exit fat woman. Exit fat chap a few minutes later, wondering why he ever leaves home.

Easter is not in the Christmas league for overindulgence in the Wogan household, but we're up there with the best of them when it comes to eggs. Once again, it's Helen Wogan's fault; she buys everybody three eggs each, and we all feel honour-bound to do the same. Up to our armpits in milk and dark chocolate, we'll still be eating Easter eggs at Christmas. Easter Sunday's the big day, the family assembled, grandsons and all, for Lady Wogan's duck. Nobody, but nobody, does roast duck like Helen: crisp, unctuous skin, meat falling from the bone, cauliflower cheese for Katherine, rich roast potatoes, crisp and browned on the outside, soft and fluffy inside. It's wonderful that our children still want to spend time with us – I hope that it's not just because of their mother's cooking.

10 April 2007

Back from the Easter break to the latest money-saving wheeze of local councils: fortnightly rubbish collections! Was it a trick of the light, or were residents not being fined last week for putting out their rubbish a few hours early, on the grounds of health, safety and vermin? Now, it's OK to store rubbish for two weeks, without causing the same problem. Still, so long as you're doing your bit to save the planet by recycling. Tim Gustard, a brilliant painter of still life, tells me that his framer decided to have a big clear-out of his workshop, filled his car with wooden frames and cardboard, and took it all off to his high-tech, brand-new recycling unit. He didn't even get through the gate. 'You can't bring that in 'ere, mate.' 'Why not?' 'Business rubbish.' 'So, what do you suggest I do with it?' 'Not my problem, mate.' The framer returned home, fuming, and rang the Eden District Council. They apologised for their employee's attitude, and told the man that he could purchase bags and stickers and put the rubbish out for weekly collection. He could put out as much as he liked, at a cost of only a pound a week. A pound a week! That's cheaper than the cost of driving to the tip, and more environmentally friendly. 'And will it be recycled?' he asked. 'Oh no, sir, it will go for landfill with the rest of the rubbish.'

Another listener's local council have kindly sent a circular to householders explaining how certain items are recycled. For instance, plastic milk cartons are sent by road from Sussex to Bolton in Lancashire, where they're packaged, sent on to the docks, to then travel 6,000 miles by container ship to China, where they are smartly turned into plastic garden furniture, and then shipped back in containers to us. How's that for a carbon footprint? The listener thought that he'd check just how many of his household products originated in the Orient: garden chairs, radio, alarm clock, hand cream, telephone, drinking mug, books. He ordered a Chinese takeaway. At least that was made in Britain.

11 April 2007

My spies are everywhere. The shrewdly named Steve Moles is already in Helsinki, preparing the ground for the Eurofest of Fine Music. He tells me that this year's stage set is modelled on the backbone of a pike. 'The Feast of the North', the eating of said fish being fundamental to a Finn's well-being. Pike? We throw 'em back. Muddy-flavoured and bony, I'm told. The French, of course, eat them, but only after pounding seven bells out of the things, wrapping them in breadcrumbs, and surrounding them with a tasty sauce. But then, the French have proven over the years that they can, and will, eat any-thing. The fish-eating habits of our Nordic friends are a worry. Some years ago, a lovely lady named Julie Lewis gave lots of money to *Children in Need* for the doubtful privilege of accompanying me to Norway, first, to cut down the Christmas tree for Trafalgar Square, and second, to go to Hell and back – Hell being a Norwegian town. The hospitality was of the finest – dear old Pauly took out most of a reindeer herd at table – until they offered us their greatest delicacy: fish that had been well rotted underground for some weeks. We passed . . . Still, I'm looking forward to Helsinki, and seeing what the Finns can do differently, and better, than last year's marvellous Greek production in Athens. Your Nordic has a strange sense of humour – might be due to his diet.

13 April 2007

A regular, if demented, correspondent, Zebedee Doodah, keeps an eye for me on television programmes that I wouldn't watch if you paid me:

> *What on earth has gone wrong with the world?*
>
> *On Saturday night I tuned into* Any Dream Will Do *only to catch sight of all these wannabe Josephs blubbering on the shoulder of Sir Andrew Lloyd Grossman, regardless of whether they had passed the audition or not, and then going outside only to repeat the performance over a bemused Graham Norton!*
>
> *By stark contrast, on last night's edition of* The Apprentice, *the losing team, a bunch of feisty ladettes, when grilled about their failings by a tetchy Sir Sidney James Sugar, certainly gave as good as they got.*
>
> *Answering back, fighting their corner; indeed the eventual sackee stood up, thanked Sir Sidney, and left the board room head held high and stiff upper lip well and truly in place.*
>
> *The feminists have won!*
>
> *Sorry, I have to go now to run the wife's morning bath.*

And rightly so. 'Girl power!' as those nice Spice Girls used to say. Whatever happened to them?

Fresh news! Live Earth, the rock concerts to be held on all seven continents simultaneously to raise awareness of the environmental impact of our reckless consumption of the Earth's resources, will feature more than a hundred bands from all over our doomed planet, many of whom, such as the Red Hot Chilli Peppers at Wembley, will not be playing at home. So, an environmentally semi-conscious listener points out, that's a plane for each band, another for its entourage, a freight plane for the sound and lighting equipment, a fleet of limos and trucks to and from the airport, air-conditioned hotel suites, food and drink by the lorry-load – all multiplied by a hundred. Then, there's the huge amount of electricity needed to stage the concerts and the fuel used to transport a million fans, plus Al Gore! We're just not going to have enough wind turbines to cope.

15 April 2007

All week, we've been bombarded with the earth-shattering news of the break-up of Prince William and Kate Middleton. Iraq, Iran, Afghanistan, Gaza have all been put in their proper place by the popular press. It's whether Wills and Kate, sweethearts of old St Andrews, now tragically forced to part, will ever find true love. Royal-watchers, insiders, people close to Clarence House and Highgrove are giving us the benefit of their insights, when, of course, we know that they know no more than we do. Saunders of Bungay, as he so rarely does, puts the hullabaloo in context:

The denizens of Fleet Street have been telling us today that the break-up between Kate and William was probably the result of their differing backgrounds. This being so, the list of future entrants to the 'Find a Bride for William Contest' will be restricted to anyone from the same background. They must be:

1. *Female*
2. *Called Hapsburg, Bourbon or Hohenzollern*
3. *Next in line to a throne*
4. *Right fit*
5. *Impervious to the antics of our wonderful tabloid press.*

And then, as usual, he went too far:

Given that the White Heather Club are getting all out of order again, it's time for a repeat of the medicine we used to dish out in Tudor times.

The ruling elite would carry off a Scottish princess in order to secure their dynastic survival and the royal line. As there is now a vacancy, we can hold a tournament, and save the Union.

However, as there seems to be a bit of a dearth of Scottish female aristocrats, the tournament will be limited to the following:

1. *Lulu*
2. *Sheena Easton*
3. *Kirsty Wark*
4. *Moira Stewart (who is obviously Scottish)*
5. *Jimmy Krankie.*

Jimmy Krankie will be allowed to stand on a box and be in drag. Last one standing gets the lad.

After the winner is announced, Prince William gets a fresh horse and a day's start.

If I were Kate Middleton, I'd go for a long trek up the Hindu-Kush. The poor girl will get no peace.

18 April 2007

Watching the BBC's *Six O'Clock News* last night, we were blithely informed by a young reporter that the early blossoming of hawthorn bushes, and the appearance of swifts, was due to the unseasonal sunshine and, therefore, global warming. This girl may well be a scientist, climatologist or meteorologist in her spare time and have good reason for her sweeping assertion, but I got an email from a listener today who keeps a diary. She pointed out that eleven years ago, on Wednesday 17 April 1996, she had written: 'Saw the first swallows today . . .' Swallows or swifts – I've never been able to tell the little blighters apart – how did they know that the sun was splitting the paving stones in Blighty? There they are, swooping about their business in North Africa, and the message comes through: 'Lads, summer's started early in the UK, off we go until we see the White Cliffs of Dover.' All was revealed by another listener today: it's the lengthening hours of daylight that bring our feathered friends northwards. Nothing to do with temperature.

Lord Harbinger of Doom is our resident sceptic:

The current hype about Spring being Summer and the swifts realising the weather was good here, made me look a little

*deeper. Surprisingly we had a long period of cold springs from
1962 to 1987, with no year even reaching an average of 9 °C
(48°F in old money). That's when coal was king and CO$_2$
emissions were sky-rocketing. Presumably all the current
excitement about early sightings of wildlife is due to the fact
that things are returning to a more comfortable level after all
those cold years.*

*The hottest spring to date is that of 1893, when it was
10.2 °C average, a full 1.6°C warmer than Spring 2006. Next
hottest was 1945.*

*The strange thing is, I can't think there were many 4x4s
on the roads in 1893. Or perhaps it was down to horse
emissions . . .*

Come now – nobody wants the facts. If it's a scorching summer, keep an eye peeled for the first vulture.

20 April 2007

Some bright spark, claiming to be a Minister of Something or
Other has just come up with the bright idea of 'tagging' the
elderly. Stand well back – the TOGs are on fire!

*That's it then! The last straw has been delivered to the camel's
back. Some lickspittling poltroon has suggested that old people
ought to be tagged when they are out and about. I did not do
my bit in the recent unpleasantness against the Teuton for this
ignominy to be heaped upon us.*

The proposers of this nonsense claim it is for our security.

BALDERDASH. It is revenge for all those years when we kept them in check: it is mean and nasty.

STEWART EGLIN,
KIRKCALDY

I for one am very much in favour of putting a tag on TOGs. It would mean that when I wake up in the morning after a heavy night of drinking, I would have a little card to tell me who I was and where I live.

YOURS SINCERELY,
LOU SMORALS

Tagging elderly

Liz Magee took things to the limit: 'The Department of TOG tagging is to launch their new scheme with a "Seniors Tagging Week". The public are asked to take part, and there will be prizes for the most oldsters tagged. Volunteers are asked to collect their nets from the Department and to use the humane "netting" process, used by the RSPB. Volunteers should lurk outside known elderly gathering places – bridge clubs, Legion Halls, snugs, etc., and employ nubile lasses to drive the old geezers into their nets. The tagging process is simple and painless. Remember, it is for their own good.' Ouch!

22 April 2007

The hot spell is bringing out the big boys among the flora and fauna. People are being terrorised by bees the size of birds, which delight in infiltrating closed spaces like cars and kitchens and frightening the liver and lights out of the more sensitive TOG:

> *In a traffic jam one of those bees*
> *Buzzed in my window to escape the breeze*
> *Landing lightly on my shoulder*
> *It took its chance to get a bit bolder*
> *Niftily crawling inside my shirt*
> *Underneath my seat belt it started to hurt*
> *So mid traffic snarl-up it deigned to bring*
> *All the delights of a grade-one sting*
> *How to remove the pesky critter*
> *When nowhere could I see a Kwikfit fitter*
> *Nothing for it but to divest*
> *So myself of shirt and me with no vest*
> *So three lanes of traffic took a massed double-take*

As out of the window my pink shirt I did shake
Which brings me to the point of this 'pome'
To explain my recent topless drive home.

THE OLD MAN OF BANGOR TOWN

Never mind the bees! Have you seen the wasps?
One, the size of a Vulcan bomber, has just carried out a
dawn raid on the kitchen. It's all well and good whilst it's in
view but it's just disappeared so I've escaped and shut the door
– thus putting myself out of reach of refreshments and vittles!
If this is the last email I write, please make it known I
fought to the last.

TANSY WHITEBYTTS

I have remarked here before on my inability to react sensibly in moments of crisis. I'm the same with creatures, whatever their size, who dare to buzz about my person. 'Sting me at your peril!' is my brave cry. I actually once ate a bee, mistaking the poor creature for a particularly tasty and crisp little piece of beef. I'm a little foolhardy when it comes to food.

24 April 2007

As of the other day, any alien or person of a foreign persuasion wishing to enter Britain's apparently desirable shores has to answer pertinent questions that will leave their objectives and allegiances in no doubt. Questions such as: 'In which year did Julius Caesar invade this country?' Not the easiest, and a question most of the indigenous population couldn't answer – as well as being of doubtful relevance. Luckily for us, a listener has carried out a Trend Analysis Study, paying special attention to the specific demographic critical path, and taking into particular account more recent current affairs that affect the nation. This study, at the taxpayers' expense, has narrowed down the Immigration Test to just three vital questions:

1. Can you bat?
2. Can you bowl?
3. Can you catch?

Sorted.

Who the Sam Hill came up with the bright idea of advising Americans that if they are lucky enough to meet Her Majesty the Queen on her upcoming visit Stateside, they must first address her as 'Your Majesty', and then as 'Ma'am', as in 'jam'. For heaven's sake! Americans have never heard of 'jam'. The poor saps call it 'jelly'. And jelly's 'jello', crisps are 'chips', while 'chips' are 'French fries', and then there's 'aragula', 'cilantro', 'squash' and 'bayzil'. And could somebody warn Her Majesty about 'grits'?

Oh, and it's Helen and my wedding anniversary today . . . forty-two years ago we got married in the rain at Rathmines Church, Dublin. It was filmed by RTE, the Irish Television Service, and Jonathan Ross showed it the last time I was on his show. The crowds had turned out – as they do for everything in Ireland – and, because it was raining, they followed us into the church. Standing in, and on top of, the pews and up the centre aisle of the big church, they joined in the ceremony merrily. We had to fight our way out in the end, but it all added to the wonder of the day. Helen's father threw a grand levée for us in a hotel in Portmarnock on the sandy shores of the Irish Sea, the rain held off for the photos, the 'craic' was mighty, and we took off in a happy haze, to honeymoon in Torremolinos. I had to strip off in the gents at Heathrow to rid myself of the half-hundredweight of confetti that the ushers had shoved roughly into every orifice. It was late when we arrived at the hotel, and when we got to our bridal suite, they'd given us two single beds . . . Seems like yesterday . . .

25 April 2007

To the College of Heralds to meet our friend Robert Noel, Lancaster Herald, and his assistant, Sarah Flower. Today's the day I get my armorial bearings, my crest, my badge of honour, as a Knight of the Realm. I wouldn't have known the first thing about this, if it hadn't been for my dear friends and neighbours Sir Jack and Lady Page. We share a libation and a mouthful of food together from time to time, and about a year ago Sir Jack told me he was going about getting his escutcheon, with the kindly help of Robert Noel. Jack put me in touch, and today is the culmination. With Robert's help the crest has been designed, meticulously painted and beautifully inscribed. There is the knight's helm, four shamrocks to represent our four children (including Vanessa, who died), three rose bushes, to remind us of Rose, my mother, and Helen's mother, Ellie, who hailed from Sligo, where the rose is part of the county crest. There is a chevron of ermine, which speaks of the grocer's profession, for both Helen's and my father were grocers. There are three martlets from the old Wogan crest, and below the motto hangs the medal of my honorary knighthood, the KBE. The motto reads *Esse Quam Videri* which I roughly translate as 'To be what I seem to be' – not a bad motto to which to aspire.

Below the citation hang two great seals, those of the Commanders of the Royal Victorian Order. It has taken almost a year to complete, it's beautiful, and Helen and I will treasure it – always.

26 April 2007

Woke up in agony in the middle of the night with cramp in both legs. One is bad enough, but two! I was in such pain, I could hardly get both feet on the floor, and then one went from under me, and I cracked to the ground on my left side, banging into the bedside table. I haven't fallen down for years, and it was a real purler, all sixteen stone of me going down like a ton of bricks. Nothing broken, I dragged myself back into bed, but it was painful, and the morning light showed spectacular bruising from hip to knee.

Naturally, pluck and grit being my two middle names, I presented myself the following morning at my place of work, to be greeted by hearty laughter at my limping gait, and no sympathy whatever from the listener, when I recounted my tale of woe. 'Big girl's blouse' was the least of it, along with exhortations to 'be a man' and opinions that I 'didn't know the meaning of the word "pain"'. I think someone even said, 'You men should have the babies,' and I finished more hurt than I'd arrived. Others seemed to think that it was some kind of joke.

As you rise from your truckle bed
With sleepy eyes and drowsy head
On Nature's law you can depend.
It's the cramp that gets you in the end!

While on the terrace birdies wait
To chirp and chuckle at your fate
Agonised screams through the dawn light rend.
It's the cramp that gets you in the end!

Catapulted window-wards
Suddenly approaching hard floorboards
That's superannuation's trend.
It's the cramp that gets you in the end!

Who else but 'Crooky' from Bangor. I'm supposed to have no feelings, of course . . .

27 April 2007

My friend Michael Smith is chairman of the Royal Blind Society and has asked me to open a new wing of the Society home, the Bradbury Hotel in East Preston, West Sussex. Radio show over, Dennis and I head for Sussex-by-the-Sea. I confess I'm not familiar with the beauties of the county, although my friend Doctor Bev daily sings its praises as a native; it was the place where he did his courting and got married. Bev's an old romantic, so I take his effusions with a grain of salt, but on this lovely day Sussex showed me all her beauty – the little villages, the endless fields, the rolling Downs. We pass Arundel Castle, where later on in the year we will be helping David and Carina Frost's three sons celebrate a joint birthday.

They're waiting for me when I arrive at the Bradbury – supporters, helpers, the blind, for whom it is such a haven of tranquillity and rest. The rooms are lovely, comfortable, each with its own bathroom. It's a place where the blind may come for a week or more, a couple of times a year, to escape the rush and bustle of their everyday lives, to be cared for, looked after, to rest and restore their spirits. I declare the new wing open, and we all sit down to a jolly lunch. It's a day full of charm and laughter, and I travel back through the beautiful countryside feeling as if I've done some good today.

29 April 2007

Sunday lunch with our dear friends Peter and Jackie Alliss in their lovely house near Hindhead, ablaze with rhododendrons and alive with chickens, Weimaraner dogs and various Allisses. We love coming to Bucklands, it's like coming home, the warmth, the smiles, the sheer bonhomie that Peter and Jackie so effortlessly generate. Also, Jackie can cook, and the old boy keeps a decent cellar. So good to see Sara, their lovely, smiley, full-of-personality daughter, so happily married to Jonathan. We've been friends for ages, the Allisses and Wogans; we've seen our children born, grow up, go through the agonies of adolescence, come out the other side, go to university, get married. We've so much in common that we just seem to fold into each other, comfortable, with a deep mutual affection. I'm honoured to be godfather to Henry, their youngest. He's in his twenties now, but I remember easing his teething pains with a dash of port on my little finger.

There's admiration there too, of course, for Peter, the nonpareil, the sports commentator against whom all others are measured. Matchless, effortless with the easy grace that he brought to his golf. Jackie, Justice of the Peace, running charity golf days with similar Alliss charm and calm. And she flies aeroplanes . . . The lunch was delicious; I can't remember a word of what we talked about, but we laughed, ate and drank as we always do, and I hope always will, while we have breath in our bodies.

1 May 2007

Last night was Sony Radio Awards night at the Grosvenor House Hotel, the twenty-fifth anniversary of Britain's most important radio awards, the veritable Oscars of the microphone. I was honoured that the committee asked me to present the evening along with the regular compère, Paul Gambaccini. I've known Paul for thirty years or more, and he has never lost his New York accent. I listened the other day to a recording of mine from the Seventies, on Radios 1 and 2, and I've certainly lost much of the Irish accent I came to Britain with.

The Grosvenor House is a huge venue, with a great sweeping

staircase, and more than 1,000 eager winners, losers, producers, presenters and executives jammed around their tables for radio's biggest night of the year. It's a bit of an ordeal, presenting a show in front of your peers, but they were kind, laughing and applauding in the right places. It's a long evening, particularly if you haven't won anything, but what I like best about it is the tribute it pays to the local radio stations, both BBC and commercial. National radio gets enough attention, and it's only proper that the talents and creativity displayed by broadcasters on smaller stations to smaller audiences be applauded and rewarded. The presenters and producers of these local radio stations are the national broadcasters of the future; they have to be brought forward and encouraged.

I won one of the first Sony Awards, twenty-five years ago, and last year, the Gold Award. That was probably for long service. Good to see Chris Evans win not one, but two awards this year – it helped to make it another big night for Radio 2, with Mark Radcliffe another winner.

Meanwhile, over at the Deserted Doughnut, BBC TV Centre, they're recording the new *Paul O'Grady Show* for Channel 4 and I'm there at midday for a recording that starts at one. As always, he makes it a pleasure to join him on stage. Sophie Ellis Bextor was on as well, with her strange beauty and the longest legs in Christendom. She spoke of the little baby for whom she gave up pop music for two years and his lovely red hair. 'A ginger,' I said, by way of a light-hearted comment. Sophie took it badly, and so did Paul O'Grady, who had red hair himself when he was a boy. Honestly, I'd no idea it was an insult . . .

2 May 2007

Show over, at ten in the morning I'm down at Bentley's, Richard Corrigan's brilliant restaurant in Swallow Street, off Regent Street. Richard has been one of Britain's top chefs for many a year now, and a winner recently of a television competition to cook for the Queen. His speciality is fish, and he's a great supporter of his native Ireland's produce. This morning he's cooking the full Irish breakfast, for a series that he's doing for RTE, the Irish Television Service, and I'm the guinea pig. Mind you, it's no hardship to sit down to a plate of sausages, bacon, mushrooms, eggs, beans and Irish wholemeal bread. Oh, and there are kidneys as well. I've got to cook them for the television. There's no such thing as a free breakfast . . .

Not long now to the Eurovision in Helsinki, and excitement and anticipation are building to what can only prove to be an epochal anti-climax. All is not sweetness and light, however. An episode of *Dr Who* is to be postponed to facilitate the Song Contest transmission. Not everyone is delighted: 'So, instead of watching oddly dressed aliens acting strangely and speaking in strange tongues, we have the opportunity of watching oddly dressed aliens acting strangely and *singing* in strange tongues', surely missing the point of this splendid international musical bonding of the nations from the Atlantic to the Urals, as they demonstrate their ancient alliances and hatreds. Don't talk to me about Daleks.

4 May 2007

The council elections. As usual nobody gives a tinker's curse in England, but in Scotland it's a different story. Scotland for the Scots is the William Wallace war cry, although there appears to be some confusion according to Sally Forth:

We've had the non-arrival of postal votes, or their late arrival with postal voters then being told the only way to vote in time is to send it by courier;

around a hundred thousand spoiled ballot papers because bemused voters have managed to put their cross – or their number – in the wrong column;

or folded their ballot paper despite the DO NOT FOLD instructions;

or put it in the wrong box;

or put it in the right box the wrong way round;

and in several places counting was suspended because the new computer scanning system kept going wrong . . .

And from Sir Russ Cloud, of Ayrshire:

In the run-up to the election in Scotland, one party outdid all the others in terms of the volume of printed leaflets through the door and the number of plasticised posters attached to lampposts with plastic cable ties. Which party? The Green Party. Is it me?

South of a line from St Albans to the Wash, things proceeded in their normal phlegmatic fashion:

'Is it me? I didn't have my polling card with me yesterday but the clerk said she only needed my address. She checked the list and said, Marielyn Hollowell. But, I retorted, what if it isn't me? Ah, chipped in another clerk, we'd ask you some questions. Intrigued I asked how they would know whether they needed to ask probing questions. Easy, you have an honest face, he retorted.

So much for heightened security and efforts to stamp out chicanery at the ballot box. Or, I ask you again, is it just me?'

I wish they wouldn't keep asking me that. It's *them*, not us. We're all right . . . aren't we? . . .

Last week it was pomegranates that were going to keep us all alive forever. This week, it's cherries. It seems like only yesterday that sunshine was the secret of rude good health, but this week a gnome of Zurich warns that the old knotted handkerchief on the head is no longer adequate protection from the sun's lethal rays. And you can forget that old Panama hat of yours – it's as much use as sunglasses in a rainstorm. Professor Lagertop of Zurich (whom God protect) will accept nothing less than a heavy woollen balaclava on the bonce, having first painted yourself with factor 50 sunscreen, so that you look like an Australian cricketer, or Marley's ghost. In ninety degrees of heat, you must wrap up in interlock vest, woolly jumper, denims or heavy cords, lest the merest chink of sunlight penetrate to your lily-white skin. If only we could blot out the sun altogether.

5 May 2007

It's the May bank holiday, and our friends Tom and Margaretta Lynch have flown over from Ireland for the weekend, so it's time for me to display to friends and family my mastery of the barbecue. So far, the doomsayers' predictions that global warming is going to do us all up like a kipper are not going to plan. April was delightful, sunny and warm, but May has so far been a soggy disappointment for those of us looking forward to a bit of climate change. It is my intention to barbecue the beast, whatever the weather, but Helen has laid the table in the conservatory, so that we may eat, drink and be merry out of reach of the sun's harmful rays. The fact that it's raining cats and dogs may have something to do with it also.

The trouble with our house is that there are too many cooks, and no sooner does son Mark arrive than he takes my shiny implements from me and commandeers the barbecue. My father, Michael, used to do the same thing when I was a lad, first placing a hammer, chisel or screwdriver in my hand, and then quickly taking them away, leaving me with a feeling of inadequacy in the presence of inanimate objects, which is with me to this day. Why do you think Helen changes the plugs in our house? I'm barely allowed to put out the bins.

Butterfly lamb is our meat of choice, and, I grudgingly admit, beautifully cooked by Mark. On the other hand, he used to be the executive chef at the Groucho Club, so should we expect anything less? He has brought along his lovely Susan, and grandson number two, Harry Wogan. Although he's only six months old, to call him 'Little Harry' would be a mistake. The boy's a bruiser. He'll be about two metres tall and one metre wide, before he's ten. Freddie Cripps, grandson number one, is here with his mother, Katherine, my daughter. He's a spare and muscular bloke of two and a half years, who runs like the wind. His father, Henry, was a fine rugby player and an athletics champion, so I have high hopes of both boys turning out for Ireland at rugby, Freddie in the centre, Harry at lock. Watch me cling to the wreckage long enough to see it.

Henry's not with us today – he misses a lot of family dos as he runs his and Katherine's pub and restaurant near Windsor. It's been a runaway success since they opened nine months ago, but the food and beverage business is a most demanding one, and Henry's on the go from morning to night, with no days off. Still, it would be something else if it was empty of customers. We took Tom and Margaretta there last night, and they loved it. I know, I know, what else are they going to say? But they know their stuff – they run a successful food business themselves, in Dublin. Tom liked the warm potted shrimps so much, he's taking a pot back to his friend Cathal. You can't take scissors, tweezers, liquids, gels or paste on a plane these days, but Tom's confident he can get the potted shrimps through.

9 May 2007

Like the Horse of the Year Show, or income tax, the Eurovision Song Contest comes around every six weeks – or so it seems. This year we're Helsinki-bound because the outlandish super-Goths, Lordi, carried off the prize last year for Finland. People ask me why I continue to commentate on the Eurovision each year, while most of my senses are still intact. Then they tell me that, in their considered opinion, the thing is, and always has been, rubbish. As if I didn't know! Magnificent, ridiculous, increasingly camp rubbish. Which is why I love it – me, and the eleven million viewers in the UK who watch it every year. And there isn't a radio and TV presenter in the land, including Jeremy Paxman and John Humphrys, who wouldn't tear the commentator's microphone from my grasp, if they got half a chance. And what wouldn't the Americas or the Antipodes give, if they could stage such a contest.

There are fringe benefits, of course, I will not pretend otherwise. Early in the year, our executive producer, or as he likes to be called, GB One, the charming Kevin Bishop, whom I have worked with since he was a snivelling floor manager, and who directed *Wogan* for the first year and a half of its exalted existence, took off to the Eurovision's location on the pretext of making sure that everything would be hunky-dory with the production, and to liaise freely with his fellow executives from all four corners of the European Broadcasting Union. No easy task – there are at least forty-four of them these days. The real reason Kevin goes to the venue is actually to spy out the land for hotels and restaurants, and a discerning job he makes of it. Not that he gets a chance to enjoy a soft bed or a decent meal, once the mad merry-go-round gets started. It used to be a pretty decent jolly for the producer, when there was just a final, and fifteen to twenty nations taking part. I distinctly remember Bishop coming to dinner one evening, and actually going to bed, in the quondam days. Nowadays, with forty-four countries taking part, endless rehearsals twice daily, a semi-final on Thursday, which BBC 3 transmits, and the grand finale on Saturday, which half the world watches – mainly aghast – the conscientious, tireless Kevin Bishop doesn't get a moment to himself. Except when he sits with me in the commentary box, pretending to laugh at my platitudes. Even then, he takes it upon himself to provide me and Ken Bruce – giving his all for Radio 2 in the box next door – with sustaining beverages, which he usually smuggles in a couple of days previously under the noses of security. A great man.

Eurovision

We arrive at Helsinki airport in the evening, but it's as bright as midday, and will continue to be until about eleven o'clock. We're going to be woken by a particularly early dawn as well, this far north. The sun is shining, but on first inspection Helsinki doesn't look any great shakes – dull, uninteresting buildings and dull-looking inhabitants, reminding me of another Eurovision location, Oslo, where the anorak is king. I'm hardly through the door of the hotel before I'm set upon by a family of Greeks, who seem to have put up camp in the foyer. About twenty of them, already decked out in the blue and white colours of their native land, here to cheer on the Greek entry, a vivacious fellow, educated by the Jesuits in

London. With the sensitivity that characterises the EBU, the entire Turkish deputation is also in this hotel, at the other end of the foyer. They're going to get me as well, as soon as the Greeks have drained me of all emotion.

Kevin the restaurant spy has selected a convenient spot for dinner, and we repair there with a family: mother, father, daughter, who have donated an enormous amount of money to *Children in Need* for the doubtful privilege of accompanying myself, Bruce, Barrowlands Boyd and Bishop to the Song Contest. Lovely people, who wish to remain anonymous, but whose company is a real pleasure. The restaurant, like Helsinki, is a disappointment on first sight, but the food is excellent. The wine list is passed to me, which just shows you how much the others know, and I recoil from it in shock. The cheapest bottle is thirty-five quid, and a perfectly ordinary Côtes du Rhône is fifty smackers. I do the best I can, but at these prices, the bill takes on Ramsay-esque proportions. It appears that all alcohol in Finland, and the rest of Scandinavia, must be purchased in an official government liquor store – there are no wholesale prices for restaurants or hotels, which must buy the booze at the same retail price as the ordinary Finn in the street. The inevitable mark-up in eateries puts the price of plonk through the roof. Looks like water from here on in . . . How am I going to get through the Eurovision?

10 May 2007

What a treat! I don't have to get up till half-seven! Who am I kidding? There's a two-hour time difference between here and

Greenwich, and my body clock knows that it's really half-five in the morning. He who never sleeps is waiting for me in the hotel foyer, old Bright-as-a-Button Bishop, and I'm surprised that we don't have to step over sleeping Greeks and Turks, but off we go to Finnish Radio. The inevitable security check, and then a charming woman leads us down endless corridors to our broadcasting studio. I hope she's going to lead us back to the front door when we've finished, otherwise we're going to spend the rest of the week trying to find our way out. In my experience, it's the same the whole world over – Istanbul, Athens, Kiev, Tallinn – every national broadcasting headquarters in the world has been designed by a rabbit. Or in the case of the BBC, by a mole, for you never see daylight.

After my glorious return to Radio 2, I spent the next twelve years of early mornings looking at a brick wall. I tried to pretend it was the façade of Bert Birt's Bistro, the playground and watering hole of BBC middle management, when the long day's meetings were over, but I fooled nobody. The wall's not there any more, and neither are the studios. They've been razed to the ground, and one day, in a much longer time and at far greater expense than anyone has anticipated, a new Broadcasting House will rise. And I'll take whatever odds you like that it will have endless corridors, and all the broadcasting studios will be below ground. Lest I be accused of unfairly biting the hand that feeds, Radio 2's new home, Western House, has studios through whose windows you can see daylight. In my little haven of happiness, Studio J, the windows look out on a panorama of air-conditioning units and dreary rooftops, but let's be thankful for small mercies: I can see the sky, and the odd pigeon coughing his way towards Trafalgar Square and breakfast. I've never understood why designers of radio studios invariably place them down dingy corridors or basements, where the sun never shines. I may be only fooling myself, but I really believe that being able to see the sky, even on dark winter mornings, lifts my spirits and performance. How can watching the dawn break over London not be more uplifting than the claustrophobia of four walls and artificial light?

It's Thursday, and I'll be damned if I'll go to the commentators briefing at the arena, venue for the Contest. I know my Finnish: 'Hey' ('Hello') and 'Hey, hey' ('Goodbye'). The rest of them – Romanian, Serbian, Russian, Hungarian and the others – I'll pronounce confidently and probably wrongly, but who's going to contradict me? So, the Wogan family takes a tour of old Helsinki in the sunshine. Yes, the gang's all here – well, most of them; Katherine, my daughter, is pregnant, and is the only one who will have to suffer my commentary at home in the UK. Alan, Mark and the present Lady Wogan have joined me, Alan and Mark at their own expense, Helen at mine. It was ever thus . . . And now that we have a chance to get away from the hotel, we see that Helsinki is really rather a lovely town. Away from the main drag with its crowds and trams, there are parks and lakes, and a charming harbour, from which Finns escape every weekend to Tallinn, Estonia, for a decent drink at a reasonable price. There's the truly breathtaking Senate Square, with its huge white church. In preparation for the great Song Contest, a stage has been erected, where, even now, they're playing live music to a crowd sprawled on white plastic settees, and the inevitable monstrous screen, which will show the Eurovision to a 20,000 crowd the night of the final, and not many fewer for the semi-final tonight. We buy ice cream, which unsurprisingly doesn't taste of reindeer or lingonberries, the national berry of Finland, but like ice cream the world over. At lunch, we decide that 'when in Rome' etc., we will try traditional Finnish fare. Never mind, there's another dinner tonight.

A very special dinner, held in our honour at the British Embassy, by Dr Valerie Caton and her husband, David Harrison. We've been lucky enough to be invited to dinner by several British ambassadors, in Oslo, Copenhagen, Athens and Kiev – all of them memorable, relaxed, happy occasions – but wherever we go in the future, it will be hard to top Helsinki. The house itself is magnificent, with spacious rooms, and great windows that look out to the Gulf of Finland. There's a sauna and swimming pool in the basement, but we thought it might be pushing it to ask if we could sweat it off after dinner. A lovely meal, the reindeer cooked to perfection (at least, I think that's how reindeer should be cooked). The company is friendly and welcoming, a mixture of Finns and ex-pats; Dr Caton makes a charming speech, and then Keith Malin, whose wife I've had the pleasure of sitting beside. She's undoubtedly the most impressive polyglot I've ever met, speaking not only Finnish and English, but also Russian, Chinese, Spanish, French and Romanian; Keith, the husband, speaks them all as well. And they're both Eurovision fanatics, according to Keith, who after his words of welcome presents to Ken Bruce and me a handsomely bound volume, put together by the Embassy staff, entitled '52 Things You Didn't Know About Finland'. Hard luck on Ken, I get first shot at this little gem of inconsequential Finnish facts, since I'm on air before him in the morning.

11 May 2007

Generous to a fault, I'm sparing in my use of Finnish factoids, confining myself to the distance an elk travels between pees, that the Finns drink more coffee than any other nation in the world, and that, here in Nokia-land, there are more mobile phones per capita than anywhere else in the world. Proud boasts of a proud nation, reminding me of my own proud people, the Irish, who for many years thought it worth shouting that the country was snake-free thanks to St Patrick, and was the only place in the wide world where you could find shamrock. Which, under the name of common trefoil, grows everywhere.

Radio show over, and having made our way out of the corridor of Finnish Radio for the last time, we're off to the arena for the first dress rehearsal. I've endured all forty-four entries already, so, if you can believe it, to have them reduced to a final twenty-four is a blessing. Fourteen countries have qualified from last year, and ten have come through from the semi-final last night. It's not without significance that not one Western European entry has made the cut. Switzerland's entry, Monaco's, Malta's, Iceland's, Denmark's had all seemed certs to me to qualify, but the former Russian bloc has done for them.

The arena itself is an indoor stadium, used mainly for the Finnish obsession, ice hockey. It will take 20,000-plus, and there are at least 10,000 fans here for the first dress rehearsal. So, it's going to be packed for the final dress, and the big show itself, tomorrow. At over £100 a ticket, who says the Eurovision is too expensive to stage? Not the Greeks – they made several million pounds' profit out of the contest last year. The Greek production was the most spectacular yet seen, but this is going to knock all previous Eurovisions into a cocked hat: the lighting, the back projection, the staging, the precision of direction, the smoothness of the production are simply brilliant. All these rehearsals have paid off. Two hours of campery, tomfoolery, naïve choreography and pretty dreadful songs roll by, and at the end I find myself in my usual position: one of total ignorance. I have no idea which song will win. I know it will come from the former Eastern bloc countries, which over the last few years since they've entered the competition have voted solidly for each other. Old habits die hard. Over the years we've become inured to the Scandinavians voting for each other, and the classic exchange of *douze points* between Cyprus and Greece, but they were never enough to really swing the result. The Balkans, the Baltic and the central former Russian bloc have more than enough votes to really influence the result; and they certainly have, over the last seven years. You don't have to be Nostradamus to predict that the Song Contest will go east again this year, and I say as much in my column for the *Sunday Telegraph*, also anticipating the usual shouting from the British public as the votes come in. Such prescience . . .

12 May 2007

The Greek contingent have had their faces painted in the blue and white stripes of their national flag since morning, the Turks hug their little singer emotionally, the four English girls who make up his belly-dancing backing group have silver tinsel on their heads. We've met them a couple of times, and I think that tinsel's a permanent fixture – they're going to need a chisel to get it off, when they get home. A palpable sense of anticipation fills the hotel foyer, and indeed all Helsinki – for it's the big day! The final doesn't start until ten in the evening Finnish time, so Helen, Alan and Mark are coming to the final dress rehearsal at two in the afternoon. The arena's packed for the rehearsal, and it might as well be the final itself, such is the excitement, the noise and the flag-waving of the fans. At the end, I'm my usual clueless self, and my family aren't much better, stunned by the magnificent production, the sheer size of it all, the constant roar of the audience, the endless cacophony of the music, the truly terrible depths of some of the performances. We all share a sinking feeling that a dreadful little bisexual figure in silver is so bizarre that the Eastern bloc will mistake it for entertainment, and we'll all be back in the Ukraine next year. He's the bookie's favourite, so our fears are not misplaced. Back to the hotel, get the head down for an hour or two, then back to the arena for the ten o'clock kick-off.

Well, eleven million of you saw it happen, so you won't need me to go into any great detail. A quaint little troll from Serbia, with a menacing backing group of female wardresses, won the day. Marija Serifovic, decent singer, 'Prayer', not a bad song. It did help the Serbian cause that every country from the former Yugoslavia that could vote – Slovenia, Croatia, Montenegro, Macedonia and Bosnia – all awarded their neighbour the magic *douze points*. It's hardly worth mentioning that the people of Croatia and Bosnia in particular, in view of recent history, and indeed the Second World War, must have had an extraordinary change of heart tonight. The Swedes did their usual 'and twelve points – for our good friends, the Finns'.

France, the UK and Ireland brought up the rear. It's a position with which we're growing familiar, and we've deserved no better for the last few years. So, there's an inevitable taste of sour grapes, when we protest about the bloc-voting. We haven't been good enough to get a vote anyway. The British papers will be full of protest tomorrow, but it will all happen again next year, unless the European Broadcasting Union get a grip. One obvious step in the right direction would be to allow only those countries that qualify for the final to vote; it's always been a nonsense to give a vote to the non-qualifiers. But, if I know the EBU, they'll be reluctant to disturb the goose that lays its yearly golden egg. After all, it's only the UK, Germany, France and Spain that are complaining. Mind you, they are the major contributors to the thing. Roll on next year, and Belgrade . . .

13 May 2007

Kevin Bishop, Alan Boyd, Ken Bruce, Alan and Mark Wogan and the good people who gave the mighty donation to *Children in Need* are leaving for London, but I'm on holiday as from today, and Helen and I are taking the opportunity of Helsinki's proximity to St Petersburg in Russia to fly there for a few days to visit somewhere we've always wanted to go. At Helsinki Airport we bump into the Irish contingent – fans, supporters, the RTE people – who are leaving for Dublin. I have my photograph taken with many of them, and, apart from the RTE folk, who've dealt with triumph and disaster in the Eurovision over many a year, they're all crying 'Foul', 'I can't believe it, we came last!', 'How could our song be last?', 'All those Eastern bloc countries voting for each other!' There's no place for the sweet voice of reason. 'But it was the worst song, and the worst performance.' They don't believe it, they won't believe it, they can't believe it. Yes, there was an even bigger amount of rubbish than usual, but the three last songs – France, UK and Ireland – were certainly among the worst entries. Try telling anybody in France, Ireland and, yes, the UK, that.

The obvious answer to our dilemma and, unless we can select a much better standard of song, the only way we can drag ourselves off the bottom of the heap is for the former Western bloc, or NATO, to join hands and vote for each other. It's the Cold War all over again. What about building a wall?

A short flight to St Petersburg, but the bustling Finnish hostesses manage to serve everybody with drinks and food in an hour, and then we're landing on Russian soil, and the sun is shining. Of course, it takes twice as long as the flight to get through Russian security and customs, but as we finally exit, a charming young lady greets us. Maria is twenty-seven, a fine arts graduate, mother of a five-year-old daughter, speaks perfect English and will be our guide for the next five days. We sweep along the broad boulevards, past the magnificent memorial to the siege of Leningrad and endless blocks of apartment buildings, until we come to the city itself, and the great Nevsky Prospekt, the wide, seemingly endless street that is the heart of the city. Maria and our driver deposit us at the Grand Hotel Europe, and promise to be back for a tour of the city the next morning. The Grand is no misnomer. They don't build hotels like this any more. Sweeping staircases, huge chandeliers, broad corridors, ornate rooms with high ceilings, and a dining room like a cathedral – cavernous, with a magnificent art nouveau stained-glass window, and a stage, on which a harpist plays at breakfast time, and a pianist, violinist and singer entertain at dinner. Built before the Revolution, it still evokes the glory and lavish excess of the Russia of Romanovs, Orlovs and Yusopovs.

Our first meal is in the famous Caviar Bar, with its iceberg of vodkas. Which one would we like to taste? As if we could tell one vodka from the next. It's ice-cold and slips down a treat with the caviar selection: Sevruga, Oscietra, Beluga. We love caviar – it's one of the family's excesses at Christmas – but this is the first time we've been able to compare and contrast the three great types. The Sevruga's lovely, the Oscietra's better – but from now on, it's Beluga for me! I'll have to sell my house, of course . . .

14 May 2007

The sun shines through our huge bedroom windows, and it's up and out of the grand doors of the Grand, to our guide Maria and our driver. We've picked a perfect day for a tour of the city, and I know we're going to get the works from Maria. She's off, like something that's been wound up, as we get in the car, and for the next few hours we get the whole lovely city, in every tiny detail. She must have an aqualung hidden about her dainty person, because she never draws breath. Yet, among the descriptions of bridges, parks, churches and palaces, we learn more about her: a young mother, highly educated and intelligent, with perfect English, a comprehensive knowledge of art, her city and Russia, yet struggling to make a life for herself and her child. Up early every morning to cross the city with her young daughter because she doesn't like the nursery school close to where they live now, a little flat on the opposite side of town. Her husband has a poorly paid job, she works from dawn to dusk, fetching and carrying her daughter, living from hand to mouth, hoping she can save enough money for a holiday for her daughter and herself.

Yet, compared to most who live here, she's well off. The palaces that line the river and canals, with their magnificent, crumbling façades, house families four and five to an apartment, sharing a kitchen and a bathroom. Perestroika has yet to benefit the ordinary citizen of St Petersburg. It's ironic that Lenin's Revolution of 1917, which started here – it was then called Petrograd, subsequently became Leningrad, before returning by popular vote to its original name – set out to rid Russia of the Romanovs, Orlovs, and the ridiculously wealthy elite who ruled a starving population. Yet, here we are, ninety years later, with the great mass of the Russian population still poor, and the money – more money than even that of the Romanovs – still in the hands of a few, the oligarchs, who, just in case another Lenin rears his head, live in London, Paris, Geneva – anywhere but Russia.

The bridges, the canals, the domes of the churches and cathedrals glitter in the sun: the Church of Spilled Blood, multi-domed, like a huge gingerbread cake from a fairytale. We enter the golden-domed St Isaac's Cathedral; there's a choir singing, a tall young man is kissing every icon in turn, mothers are having their children blessed by the priests. One of the priests leads the choir in the magnificent, rumbling notes that characterise the Russian basso profundo. It's all ridiculously romantic and touching, for this is a religion that would not die, that survived persecution and Stalin's pogroms, and still lives in these churches and this people.

We enjoy a delicious Italian meal in Rossi's in the Grand Hotel. How is it that they can cook foreign food, but not their own? The food is less expensive than in London, which is not saying much, but the wine list is monumentally expensive – an ordinary Pinot Grigio about £40. Wines from the owner's, Jim Sherwood, estate in Italy are astronomical.

15 May 2007

Breakfast in the cathedral that is the Grand Hotel's dining room; a harpist gently plucks her strings. The buffet looks delicious but, like all buffets, flatters to deceive. Then there's the hot food: you can't fry bacon and cover it afterwards, it ends up a soggy mess, and those sausages look dangerous. They remind me of a Sunday morning long ago when I cooked the full Irish breakfast (bacon, egg, sausages, black pudding) for Mum and Dad and brother Brian, after Mass. 'Well, son,' says the Da, 'we won't get ptomaine poisoning from these sausages.' So – they were a tad overdone, I'll admit . . . A chef cooks eggs in a corner of the Great Room. Scrambled, we order. A mistake. This man knows as much about scrambling eggs as my arse knows about snipe-shooting, to use a well-worn Irish phrase.

Outside, the Nevsky Prospekt is sluiced with rain, but several beribboned lackeys lead us to our car, and there's Maria, and Sergei, our driver. Even from a distance I can see her lips moving, and as I amble into earshot, I hear her say, 'Today, we go to the Hermitage.' Indoor work, thank goodness, for the rain is drumming down. A good job we picked yesterday for the city tour.

We'd seen the Hermitage from across the great river Neva, but up close, it's huge, overlooking a magnificent square. As Tom Master, in his excellent guide, says, 'There are art galleries, there are museums, there are the great museums of the world, and then there is the Hermitage.' Pointless for me to try to describe this unrivalled collection of art treasures housed in the magnificent palace from which the Romanovs ruled Russia. If you haven't seen it, you must – just as you must see this most beautiful city, perhaps the most beautiful in the world. The vastness of the palace, its magnificent rooms, its collections of everything from Egyptian pottery to Bronze Age jewellery, is breathtakingly impossible to take in, but for me it's the paintings that put the tin hat on it. So much for London's National Gallery; this is room after room of Rembrandt, Rubens, Matisse, Picasso, Van Gogh – every great Impressionist and post-Impressionist who ever lived. We exit the Hermitage three hours later, but we could be there for a week, and still not see everything.

Back in the hotel where Tchaikovsky spent his honeymoon, we order a snack. Another mistake. The avocado's like a brick, the prawns are as dangerously undercooked as the sausages at breakfast. Russian cooking is not yet at the glasnost stage.

And yet, following a recommendation from our friends at the Helsinki Embassy, tonight we've had a meal that would have been distinguished in the best Parisian bistro; honest French bourgeois cooking, at the Bistrot Garçon. So much for the Revolutions – French and Russian.

18 *May* 2007

Flew back from St Petersburg yesterday, full of the sights we've seen – Peter the Great's Peterhof Palace, with its amazing cascade of fountains; Catherine the Great's Palace at Pushkin with its Amber Room, its lakes and gardens, the Mariinsky Theatre, where we saw a wonderfully staged new ballet, a prelude to *The Nutcracker*, rather as the West End musical *Wicked* tells the tale of what happened before the Yellow Brick Road led to the *Wizard of Oz*. The Mariinskys' was one of the most spectacular, expensively staged musical productions I've seen. How do they afford it?

Dinner at the Greene Oak with Kevin Bishop, our executive producer from Helsinki. We felt he needed feeding up, since he didn't get a square meal in Finland.

19 *May* 2007

Kevin stayed the night, and we sent him on his way with a bacon and sausage sandwich, before we head off to Gatwick for our flight to Toulouse. We're going to spend the second week of our holiday in our house in south-west France. Let's hope the weather's as good as it was in Finland and Russia, although it's raining here today.

Airports – don't you hate 'em? Gatwick is heaven compared to Terminal One, Heathrow, but that's everyone's vision of hell. The new security regulations have played right into the hands of bureaucrats, time-servers and jobsworths. The attitude of 'security' people is a disgrace, acting like prison officers, self-important, surly, abrupt. For heaven's sake! Passengers are customers, not criminals. The good old British concept of service is alive and well at our airports. Gatwick is thronged with only two security gates open. People, having queued for at least half an hour to check in for their flights, are now queueing out to the front door to get through security. Nobody denies the need for security in these terrorised times, but couldn't a few more security gates be opened? No, it's only the passengers after all, the people who pay your wages . . .

It's raining in Toulouse when we land. Never mind, the lovely old house is still standing when we get there, and thank God the central heating's on. In the middle of May, nearly 1,000 miles south of London. Still, we have a lovely meal in our favourite restaurant, in my favourite French town, and I'm still on holiday . . . *Bon appétit*!

20–27 May 2007

A week of sunshine and showers, typical of the Gers, the French *département* where we've had a home for the past ten years. It's the second least populated *département* in the country, the tidy little villages and towns each with their *mairie*, their school, children, but no *boulangerie,* no café, no shops, few young people over seventeen. The Gers is a major contributor to France's breadbasket, and the flight from the land to the cities has taken its toll here. And Napoleonic law, which divides land and property equally among families, a splendid egalitarian idea, but one that has broken up countless homes and estates, as families grow, and the land cannot provide a living for so many people. Farms and houses are abandoned and sold – which is where the half a million or more British people who now live in France come in. There are villages in the Dordogne with more English inhabitants than French. The Gers is further south, and more off the beaten tourist track, but over the ten years Helen and I have become aware of more English accents in the supermarkets and restaurants. It has certainly benefited this area: there's a greater air of prosperity, more cars on the road, many more vineyards. But nothing has really changed in this most rural part of France; the old men still stand on their corner; people greet you in the street; the markets ignore EU rules with hot and cold meats, cheese and even fish on the same stalls; the great fields of wheat, barley, corn, rape and sunflowers sway in the breeze. The pace of life is easy and relaxed, which probably explains why the Gersoises are the longest-lived folk in France, and probably in all Europe, rather than the diet of duck, cassoulet, wine and Armagnac to which many ascribe their good health. These people's lives are ruled by the seasons; there are no targets here, no deadlines, no traffic jams, no rush.

Whenever I say that we have a house in the south-west of France, people assume that I've got a bijou residence somewhere on the Côte d'Azur, bathed in sunlight. I'm bound to say that I was expecting our French weather to be a marked improvement on the weather in Britain, being almost 1,000 miles to the south. However, 'changeable' could best describe it, and I suppose being only an hour and a half from the Bay of Biscay to the west, and the Pyrenees to the south might explain it. But we bought this house on a July day, with the sun causing the sunflowers to turn their faces to it, so I'm always a tad put out when the thunder cracks, and the lightning lights up the distant mountains. Last year, while buying a bottle or several in a London wine shop, I mentioned to the French assistant that I had a home in the Gers. 'Ah,' he said, '*les orages*' (the storms) . . . Strange that nobody mentioned them when I was buying the house.

We've eaten and drunk like kings, read, swum, Helen has painted, I've written, we've laid about and done nothing for days on end, too idle even to play a round of golf. It's a good job I don't put on weight easily.

Les orages – *the storms*

29 May 2007

Back in the old routine, the usual barrage of contumely from my unfeeling listeners on the subject of my holidays, and how long do I intend sitting in for Johnnie Walker this time? I treat these cavilling curmudgeons with the contempt they deserve, and leave the studio in a marked manner. For I have other fish to fry today – I'm off to the ASDA headquarters in Leeds. We'd never make it by train, car or plane, so it's me for Battersea, and the heliport. Up, up and away over England's green and pleasant, sunshine and showers, light and shade on the patchwork quilt below. We find a field, and are on our way to the supermarket headquarters, an hour and a half after we've left London.

Book signings are always a lottery, the main source of worry being whether the punters are going to turn up. Many a heart-rending tale is told of distinguished authors sitting alone and ignored behind a table stacked with their finest work, signing a few books dispiritedly for members of the staff pretending to be customers. Painful, chastening, and a sad reflection of the current market, which seems to cater only for the ramblings of footballers, comedians and gobs on sticks from the radio.

Hurrah! The impressive foyer of the supermarket head-quarters is full to bursting of cheery folk, who, instead of going about their lawful pursuits, are lining up to have their copies of *Mustn't Grumble* devalued by my signature. We're supposed to be there for an hour, but who'd be churlish enough to turn people away?

Two and a half hours after we arrived, we're back in the helicopter again, heading for London. Dennis drops me off at the Savoy Hotel and heads home to collect Helen, who's joining me for tonight's Royal Television Society Sports Awards. No, they're not giving me a gong at last for my sterling work at prop for Crescent College in the Munster Junior Cup in 1954, I'm handing one over.

It's a Lifetime Achievement Award, and Jonathan Martin, legendary sports producer, and now an RJS nob, has asked if I would do the honours for Peter Alliss. Assemble into a well-known phrase or saying the words 'The Pope', 'Has' and 'Balcony'. (Actually, the Pope hasn't got a balcony, he speaks from his window, but never mind.) I'm delighted and honoured to present the award to a dear friend, a brilliant broadcaster, the yardstick by whom all commentators in every sport are measured. None compare to Peter Alliss, who brings the ease, grace and wit to the microphone that he brought to golf. It's a shock to him when I turn up on stage and give him the works, but never did a man deserve an award more. Indeed, it's a thundering disgrace that he hasn't received more accolades, not just for his broadcasting, but the work he and his wife, Jackie, do for charity.

It's a long evening, but since I have to rise from my Savoy Hotel bed and make all speed to Western House, BBC Radio 2 in the early hours of the morning, Helen and I bid our fond farewells to the great and the good of the television sporting world and head for bed. A good plan, and one that might have worked, if the lights in the bedroom hadn't gone out. That was midnight, and at twenty past a man arrives with a ladder and replaces a faulty plug. Wash the teeth, take out the contact lenses, and I've got five hours' sleep ahead. I'm up with the alarm clock, Helen stirs slightly, I make for the bathroom, and find that the lights have gone out again. I dress in the dark, make my way to the foyer and complain to a man in uniform who doesn't speak English, at the front desk. Oh, and it wasn't just the lights. When vision was restored last night in our bedroom, I ordered breakfast for Helen and me, on one of those cards that you hang outside your room. I ordered my breakfast for six a.m., and Helen's for eight a.m. I confess to a nameless dread that Helen would end up with two breakfasts, and nothing for me, but I thought, Savoy, one of the world's great hotels, what can go wrong? So, I leave breakfast-less, and at eight a.m., Helen is asked by the waiter if she'd like two . . .

1 June 2007

A new month, and it hasn't started well. I've forgotten my electric shaver, and I'm not a man for designer stubble, so, while the Voice of the Balls, the Wealdstone Wonderboy, Alan Dedicoat, is dealing the eight o'clock news his usual pasting, I pick up a passing razor and shaving foam, and make for the studio powder room. Time is of the essence, and as ever when you rush things, a mistake creeps in. Only the tiniest nick, but it's just in the wrong place, at the corner of my mouth. Back in the studio just before the news ends, I slam in the Radio 2 jingle and segue a record. Time to staunch the flow. Someone finds the BBC Red Cross box, and a plaster more suitable for an elephant's knee is produced. The record ends, and with the plaster covering most of my head as well as my mouth I gamely try a few muffled words. On the other side of the glass, friends and colleagues are nowhere to be seen. They're on the floor, in hysterics. I'm bleeding to death in front of the public, and my producer, the engineer, the newsreader and the Traffic Totty are not lifting a finger. Through the gauze and what little of my mouth is open for business, I make the mistake of telling the listener of my predicament. I should have known better . . .

Staunch the flow of blood

Judging by all the blood that's about after the old chap's half crazed attempt at shaving, it's obvious that his razor is a good deal sharper than his wit!

FROM MR JACK OOZY

Oh for goodness sake man. Pull yourself together and stop behaving like a big girl's blouse. It's your own fault anyway. There is a time and place for everything, and having a shave in a BBC studio whilst in the middle of a broadcast certainly isn't one of them. Just get Dr Deadly and Nurse Taffy to whack some Germolene and an Elastoplast on it and you'll be as right as rain. I'm only being cruel to be kind you understand. The nation relies on you and we can't have you getting weak in front of the troops.

Regards

RALPHY

Following your unfortunate accident this morning, I am writing to offer myself as the Chief Negotiator for Big Payout Claims 'r Us, a company designed to 'fleece and line' the pockets of our customers. Now I understand that you were using a sharp implement to remove facial hair prior to an important engagement. So . . . some questions:

1. *Did you receive an Assessment of Risk Form before commencing the operations?*
2. *Was the position and availability of a full First-Aid Kit shown to you?*
3. *When was the age of the BBC issue bandage checked and had somebody used it first?*
4. *May I send you details of our affiliated company . . . Plastic Surgery and Reconstruction for Wrinklies based in Warsaw?*
5. *Subject to full information, I propose that we sue the BeeB for say . . . £10 Million and free luncheon vouchers for life.*

Call me on Whitehall 1212

HORATIO Q BIRDBATH
CEO

Every time I opened my mouth, the bleeding started again, not the Mae West when you're talking for a living. The hilarity of my one-time friends and producer continued unabated until the end of the programme, with not one word of sympathy for a wounded colleague. Their laughter followed me out into the street, and I fancied I saw complete strangers sniggering behind their hands even as Helen and I boarded the plane for Nice at Heathrow. I wasn't fleeing the country in shame, we were off to Vicki and Greg's wedding in Sainte Maxime. Too late for the nuptials I'm afraid, but nicely in time for the reception, in a beautiful wedding cake of a hotel, looking right across the bay to Saint Tropez. Then, down to the beach club, as the shades of night fell over the bay, a thousand twinkling lights from villas and yachts reflected on the still water.

2 June 2007

This is a five-star hotel, one of the most perfectly positioned on the Côte d'Azur, but we're not having the best of luck lately with luxury hotels. When we arrived at this sun-kissed wedding cake yesterday, eager to freshen up and drink in the delights of the wine-dark sea, we were taken to our room by a concierge, who opened the door, only to find the last occupants still in residence. At half-four in the afternoon? Downstairs, suitably chagrined, a desultory young receptionist doesn't seem overly disturbed; he offers us a complementary cocktail, and a seat in the foyer. Beyond that, he doesn't seem to have anything else to offer, obviously expecting us to sit there until the current occupants of our room have left, and the room has been cleaned, and the shades of night have fallen. Resisting the urge to shove his cocktail where the sun don't shine, I ask to see the manager. Ten minutes later, we're upgraded to a suite – result! The suite has two large windows, but surprisingly, no balcony. The windows look out over the hotel's gardens to the most beautiful view of the bay of Saint Tropez, all stately gin palaces and attendant little boats buzzing about. Only one small problem: all the seating in the suite, and the bed, is facing in the opposite direction from the view. Sit on the sofa, you've got a splendid view of the door. Lie on the bed – look! Another door! French interior design – it's in a class of its own.

4 June 2007

Back in Blighty, having endured the usual vicissitudes of airline travel or, more specifically, airport angst. The Fast-Bag Drop at Nice didn't exist, and we arrive at Heathrow to find the usual milling thousands at Baggage Claim. One of the carousels isn't working, and neither are the baggage-handlers. It's a 'go-slow', which, at the rate they normally work, is stationary. 'Wait' is the message for all flights on the information monitors. What else can you do? A paying customer, in the hands of people who don't give a toss for you or your baggage. It eventually comes up, on the wrong carousel. It's taken longer than the flight – but hey! You've been through it yourself, the hell-on-earth that is air travel.

Back in the old routine, in time for Vladimir Putin to threaten that if America has the cheek to put anti-strike missiles in his backyard, he's going to point his nuclear warheads at us in the West. So, for the last ten years, he's been pointing them in some other direction? Yeah, right.

And dear Richard Branson, possibly the greatest self-publicist and bandwagon jumper since Barnum, has leapt on to the footplate of the environmental express, the failed politicians gravy train. Richard is going to run his trains on eco-friendly fuel, which he will be importing from the Far East. Presumably, on his planes. How big a carbon footprint will that be? A TOG remarks: 'You know that the planet is in safe hands when they cut down the rainforest to grow food to use as vehicle fuel.'

5 June 2007

Welcome news that the dreaded global warming, which is providing such a damp, cold summer, is not after all going to leave us up to our oxters in snow for six months of the year by diverting the Gulf Stream. Further good news – although probably not, if you're Al Gore: the Polar icecap isn't going to melt either; it is only topped by the increasing numbers of ospreys and capercaillies – and the little-known Dartford Warbler. Not, as you may have thought a tuneful burglar, nor even a whistling footpad, but a little feathered friend welcoming our warmer winters. Then, on *Springwatch*, Bill Oddie heard the screech of a buzzard. All right, it turned out it was only Kate Humble playing a recording, but nonetheless. How much longer, you cry, before we're picking grapes on the slopes of Ben Nevis?

I've hardly divulged the good news about the return of our little friend, the Dartford Warbler, before a twitching TOG claims that it's an illegal immigrant. He says that your typical Warbler breeds in southern Europe, and the main reason the blighters' numbers have increased is that the RSPB have felled hundreds of trees in East Dorset to create a heathland habitat to suit the little impostor. The number of birds that live in trees has since plummeted. Oh, and if the reason for the increase in the Dartford Warbler is warmer winters, does that mean that when their numbers were greater in the past, we had even warmer winters?

I can't believe it: the sun is shining on the grand old edifice of Denham Golf Club, as I arrive for the annual Bucks Foundation Golf Day. The great and the good (although not necessarily at the game) gather in my name at this fine club every year to sample the finest buffet of any golf club in the land, help the less privileged of the county with their donations, and fiddle about on the course until it's time to come in for tea and the prize-giving. I haven't lifted a club in anger for about three months and, after flattering to deceive for a few holes, slump to my customary flailing about. Never mind, it's a grand carnival day in a good cause, and it's the first time the sun has shone on our endeavours for five years.

7 June 2007

An unfortunate Filipino has been shot dead in a karaoke bar because he was singing off-key, and would not desist when asked to. I expected a sympathetic reaction from my listeners to the news, but far from it. If they didn't exactly cheer, I could certainly hear muted applause. The general feeling from my crowd, a pretty representative slice of the upstanding Brit, was that the poor man got what was coming to him. This kind of random killing is pretty commonplace in Manila, where most karaoke bars have taken Frank Sinatra's 'My Way' off their playlists because of the number of people who have been shot while giving their all at it. If I'm catching the groundswell of opinion correctly, people feel there ought to be more of this kind of forthright criticism here, and most effectively on TV shows such as *Pop Idol, Any Dream Will Do* and *Grease Is The Word.* One of my more sharp-tongued listeners has suggested that this sort of gunplay might bring a welcome rigour to some of the excesses at choral evensong in his local church.

Sustaining the Far Eastern motif, it's hats off to the Japanese, clearing the rubbish left by the thousands of climbers now going up and down Everest as if it were a Magillicuddy's Reek. A listener was wondering if I had the Japanese chaps' phone number, as he'd like to borrow them for a few days to show his local council how it's done.

Another applauded the news that the Chinese are building power stations at the rate of two a week, and wondered if they could loan us their brickies for, say, a fortnight, to solve our shortage of prisons problem.

The way we live now is readily illustrated every morning in my emails:

> *Your listener yesterday – trying to email a programme sugges-*
> *tion to the BBC – struck a responsive chord.*
> *Later that morning I had cause to contact a former stal-*
> *wart of the insurance world, querying information sent*
> *through the post on behalf of a client.*
> *After the usual delays I posed my queries to the lady repre-*
> *senting the aptly misnamed Customer Services.*
> *There were further delays as the lady absorbed my questions.*
> *Trying to help, I suggested: 'Could someone ring me back*
> *and explain how they've arrived at these figures.'*
> *'No. We don't operate a telephone service.'*
> *'But you do have telephones?'*
> *'Yes, but we don't ring back.'*

'So as I've rung you, can I speak to them now?'
'No, they don't take calls.'

That was from an old sidekick of mine, Francis Klonowski. It was smartly followed by a letter from a listener who had recently moved house. He rang the NS&I to tell the Premium Bond people of his move. The reply? 'Sorry, sir, we cannot take that change of address over the phone for security reasons. I'll send you a form. What's your new address?' So, they're sending a form to him at his new address, so that he can complete it, to tell them his new address. I'm off, turn out the lights as you leave.

8 June 2007

I don't know how it came up yesterday, perhaps the Voice of the Balls, or the Taffy Traffic Totty, were behaving in an even more than usually maniacal manner, but the fine-sounding talk turned to eccentrics I have known. Obviously my family was full to bursting with half-mad maiden aunts, and most of the people I work with, as well as my friends, are not the full shilling, but pre-eminent among the loonies I have known was a Dublin character called Bang-Bang. In the Fifties and Sixties everyone in the city knew and loved him, although he'd have you jumping out of your skin as you ambled along O'Connell Street, shouting 'Bang! Bang!' From the platform of a bus.

A contemporary of mine in Dublin in the rare old times confirms my story of a beloved character.

*I'm sure most of your listeners and all of your team think
Bang Bang is a figment of your imagination.*

*But, Bang Bang was of course one of Dublin's best-known
and well-loved characters, with his cowboy stunts and shoot-
outs while swinging from the back bar of a no. 12 bus as it
careered down Camden Street or Dame Street . . . His six gun
was actually a large key, and to everyone's amusement some
times there would be a shoot-out between Bang Bang and
maybe a team of Garda, passing businessmen and bus conduc-
tors. The guards would return fire shooting from the hip,
using their index fingers, and businessmen would deliver powerful bursts of submachine gun fire from umbrellas firmly
held at shoulder height, all to the bemusement of passing
tourists or day-trippers to Dublin who were strangers to the
territory.*

*Bang Bang would then, if he thought he'd been ambushed
or outgunned, slap his rear end and – no horse! no cruelty
involved – gallop off down Dame Street into the setting sun.*

PAD CODD, BLACKHEATH

*Anybody interested in Bang Bang and all the other wonderful
characters on the Dublin scene should read* North of the
Liffey *by Bernard Neary.*

The Irish are good with 'characters' – they tolerate them, are
amused by them, even talk to them. In London, alive with
the half-mad, they are not so much tolerated as ignored, and
heaven help us if one of them speaks to you! My dear old
granny, Muds, used to sing a little ditty of a Dublin character
of her childhood: 'Billy in the Bowl, and that's it all,' went her
refrain. I thought that I'd find out who Billy in the Bowl was.

It turned out that he was a paraplegic with no legs, who propelled himself along the mean streets in a large bowl-like contraption with wheels, driving himself along with immensely strong arms. Far from lovable, he mugged and strangled the foolishly sympathetic with those strong arms. Even the Irish couldn't put that down to eccentricity, and they hung him high. Although, considering he had no legs, probably not *that* high. Still, they did make up a song about him.

11 June 2007

The fuss is still going on about the new logo for the London Olympics: 'A bizarre, strange and surreal image that looks like an explosion in a cubist's Mr Blobby factory' is the considered opinion of one art lover. I can't wait until they unveil the official mascot . . .

Still, I find it hard to get worked up – it's just not the kind of thing that causes a TOG's hackles to rise. However, the news today that the EU is going to force equal rights for women upon golf and working-men's clubs brought the nation's curmudgeons out from behind their leather armchairs. 'Does this mean that we men can have fluffy towels and perfumed soap in our club showers, two courtesy shots in pro-ams, play from the front tees, and have our fees reduced?', 'Why do women want to join a club where they're not wanted? Why not set up their own club, and ban the men?', 'Will I have to part with my titanium driver and go back to my old hickory-shaft, so as not to gain an unfair advantage?', 'Will gimmees become longer?' This last, petulant query displaying how little the old buffer knows about women; there are no gimmees in the ladies' game. 'Let's see that one in,' is all you get. And she's my wife. 'If women get equal rights on the golf course and the freedom to breastfeed in public, will this not interfere with their swing?' For heaven's sake!

Equal rights

It puts one in mind of a long-gone summer's evening (you remember them?) after an excellent round of the great game on the splendid links at Rye Golf Club. We repaired to the bar to slake our thirsts. That lovely old gent, Denis Thatcher, was already there, downing his favourite G and T, and fulminating, as ever, about the pinkos abounding in the BBC. His wife Margaret, the Prime Minister, was about her political business, kissing babies in the vicinity. Soon, we saw her official car draw up in the car park. The great lady regally entered the club, to be immediately directed to a tiny lounge down the corridor, where, if she liked, someone could get her a cup of tea. She might have been the Iron Lady, and not for turning, and Prime Minister, but rules are rules: no ladies' in the gentlemen's bar. Extraordinarily, she acquiesced, and sat calmly in the little ladies' lounge, until Denis was ready to leave. She was a club-man's wife, you see, she knew her place.

12 June 2007

One word borrows another, in my game:

Doing a shop in a supermarket, get to the till with various items, including 3 packets of 16 tablets of paracetamol, 'Can't sell you that amount,' said the assistant. 'Against regulations,' then came two bottles of Dalwhinnie (Father's Day presents) 43% proof. Assistant didn't bat an eyelid. We've got it wrong somewhere!!!!!

Immediately followed by:

I went supermarket shopping recently with a friend who had three packets of paracetamol in her basket, and was also told 'I can't sell you all three of those, so buy two and purchase the third as a separate item, on a second bill (for 16p).' She did. Sense? Nowhere to be found.

HUGO FURST

So it's sense you're after? You're in the wrong place. In fact, are any of us sure we know where we are?

I trotted off to my local pharmacy yesterday to collect a pre-scription, all bubble packed and with the days on, to ensure I take right dose, right day! Easy. But in a sleepy village in Somerset things have changed. The days were marked in French, Italian and Spanish, I think! When I complained that I had no access to a phrase book I was told to start on one cor-ner and take one each day! On complaining at their lack of patient care I was told that next time I should ask specifically for the English version when I order! I suppose then that it must be usual for Somerset (multicultural epicentre of England) to be offered this multi choice. I think I will purchase a phrase book, ready for when they change the road signs too.

Look here, do you people know how lucky you are to get any medicines at all?

I hear in the news this morning that NICE is restricting yet another useful drug in the name of saving money. Isn't it time the National Institute for Clinical Excellence was renamed? I suggest that the National Association for Stopping Treatments for You (NASTY) might be more appropriate . . . !

Bring back the old restoratives, I say. Nerve Tonic, Carters Little Liver Pills and, everybody's all-time favourite, Doctor Collis Brown's Chlorodyne. This all-purpose syrup was a sovereign remedy for whatever ailed you; colic, headache, grow-ing pains, ageing pains, toothache, bunions, colds and flu – the good Doctor's magic draught saw them all off. For it stunned all pain, just as it stunned you. You could tell people who were taking it – glazed, bemused, appearing to float, rather than walk. It saw many a family through the worst of the baby's teething troubles, it helped granddad to sleep. A boon. Why did they have to ban it – just because it contained morphine?

13 June 2007

Off to Dartmoor and Devon, for tomorrow morning's radio extravaganza comes from a ditch, and a pretty dank ditch, if the weather we experienced on the way down is anything to go by. My listeners have been glued to Bill Oddie and Kate Humble, their fur and feathers, their flora and fauna, of an early evening on BBC TV. My crowd wouldn't give you tuppence for *Big Brother*, but they lap up 'reality', when it comes in the form of 'nature' programmes, and they just love Odd Billie and Pert Kate. Frankly, I wouldn't give a tinker's curse myself about being up to my armpits in mud and lovable creatures of the wild, but Julie and Stephen Stannard of Ferring, West Sussex, donated a considerable amount of money on the 'Auction for Things That Money Can't Buy', for *Children in Need* last November, and it's only the decent thing to do to make sure that our givers don't get swept away by a flash flood, or a thundering herd of wildebeest. Anyway, someone has to protect them from Oddie.

We check in at a charming hotel on the fringe of Dartmoor, Barrowlands Boyd and myself, put ourselves outside a decent dinner and a couple of single malts, and prepare for an early night and the struggles of the morrow. Some hopes . . . in comes Oddjob and Bumble and the TV production team, plus our two benefactors, who've already been experiencing the joys of nature with Bill, Kate and the crew, and are having a marvellous time. Stop me if I've said this before, but it's always gratifying when the good people who donate so much to *Children in Need* feel that they're getting their money's worth, and more. As if we could possibly repay them . . .

14 June 2007

Up with the lark, or whatever that indigenous bird is that's making a racket outside my window, and off to Hatherleigh, a farm that has been turned into a media village, with trailers and marquees, satellite dishes and all manner of technical equipment. Quarter to seven in the morning, and the village is alive with the bustle of a live television production team. A bacon butty is thrust into my hands, and I'm led to a Portakabin – hallelujah! I don't have to rub shoulders in a ditch with some of God's slimier creatures – no, I'm interviewing Bill and Kate in the safety and warmth of our little radio studio. The programme makes its merry way through a cacophony of bird-song, bleating sheep, lowing cattle and passing lorries, which, naturally, I identify as carrying small creatures of the wild to the local abattoir. This may shock the casual listener, but will be of no surprise to TOGs, well used to our cavalier way with wildlife – the rarer the better. When the osprey returned to these shores, the Voice of the Balls opined that it might be a little stringy, with a hint of the fishy to the palate, and the late, great Pauly Walters decimated herds of reindeer on his few visits to Norway. Half an hour through the show I'm sure that there's something familiar about some of the chirruping and twittering that's going on. A glance out of the rain-dashed window of the cabin confirms my worst fears: it's Deadly, news lackey, Wealdstone Wonder-Boy and Ballmeister, all over the programme like Ronnie Ronalde in a monastery garden. The swine has followed me all the way down to Devon, to give me the benefit of his whipperwill, oriole and corncrake. I'll be damned if he'll get a clotted cream tea from me! There's no denying the 'nature' nature of the programme, particularly when the rain hammers down on the roof like a machine gun, but we didn't come all this way to sound like we do every morning from Studio J, Western House, London W1. It's refreshing to get out of the rut every so often, and this was a breath of country air.

No rest for the wicked, nor e'en the pure of heart, like myself and Deadly. As soon as today's radio show has ground to its customary anti-climactic halt, we're off to Mid-Herts Golf Club for the annual contest against the might of Ben Brown's South Herts team. Initiated originally by Pauly Walters and myself as a match between ourselves for a tiny, but intricately chased cup, the TOGs Trophy, as fine a tribute to the Taiwanese trophy-makers art as you will ever see. Then, one fine day several years ago, Ben Brown, a mighty golfer and a regular listener, suggested to Pauly, as the current Captain of Mid-Herts, that the two clubs might contend yearly for the privilege of having the TOGs Trophy grace their cabinet. The brave hearts of Mid-Herts leapt to the challenge and it's been a hotly contested meeting of titans ever since. Staged in turn by the two clubs, this year it's being fought out over Mid-Herts' rolling acres, and is of particular importance because it's the first year we'll be doing it without the laconic camaraderie of dear Pauly. This one was for him. Deadly caddies for me in his own cheery, desultory manner, which, as always, involves talking at the top of my backswing and wandering off with my clubs.

Mid-Herts edge it by a whisker, but the little TOGs Trophy has metamorphosed into a beautifully polished piece of wood, on which is mounted Pauly Walters's sacred one-iron, a club that only he, and God, could hit. A convivial dinner with players of both clubs follows, and only happy memories of our beloved Pauly: how he always wore the trousers of a suit to play golf, and then put a dark jacket over them for dinner . . . his rigid insistence on Bombay Gin, and a lime, *not* a lemon . . . those deck shoes he wore, winter and summer . . . his steadfast belief that life would be all right as long as you got a four up the first . . . the rhododendron that he nurtured out on the course, until, to his fury, a member of the ground staff cut it to bits by mistake . . . There's a new, thriving rhododendron bush in its place now, with a plaque dedicated to Paul Walters in front of it. Hard to pass, without a tear, and a smile . . .

15 June 2007

One of those weeks . . . Off to my native city of Limerick, Ireland, where the Mayor and the City Fathers are conferring on me the Freedom of the City later this evening. Much later, as it turns out . . . Myself and my fellow travellers sit powerless, trapped on board our Aer Lingus flight, as a minor engineering fault turns into a further delay, then a missed take-off slot, then an even longer delay, because an emergency had closed one of Heathrow's two runways. A plane full of

Americans, becoming ever more disgruntled with every passing hour, and special needs children becoming ever more excitable. Mary Dundon is my contact in Limerick: calm, unflappable as each delay is followed by another: 'Sure, don't worry yourself – we'll wait for you.' The plane should have taken off for Shannon at 3.15; it's five o'clock, I'm still on the ground in London, and the ceremony is due to start at six! Only the Irish could be so unmoved, so philosophical, so well mannered in the face of such a delay on such an important occasion. 'When God made time, he made plenty of it,' they say, and they believe it. We eventually take off at six o'clock, and by dint of speed and efficiency at Shannon, a stretch limo with a police escort, and a glass of champagne with the marvellous Mary Dundon, I arrive at Limerick's City Hall on the banks of the Shannon at twenty minutes to eight. Nobody says a word about my delayed arrival – not the Mayor, nor the city councillors, nor Limerick's great and good, who have all waited patiently in the wind and rain for me, nor even the distinguished artist, Dr Tom Ryan, my fellow recipient of the Freedom of the City.

We're greeted at the steps of the City Hall by an army colour party, and a piper leads the Mayor, Joe Leddin, the City Manager, Tom Mackey, the councillors, all in full ceremonial robes, Tom Ryan and myself to the conferring podium. Glowing speeches full of praise are heaped on the pair of us, before we reply in tones of suitable humility and gratitude. After that we are each presented with a rare vellum scroll that has taken craftsmen a hundred hours to inscribe, and has then been enclosed in a silver holder.

It's one of the proudest moments of my life – that my native city, this ancient historic city, should think enough of me to present me with this signal honour. Old schoolmates and friends have once again taken the time and trouble to remember someone who left them all of fifty-two years ago. Father Tom Stack, now Monsignor, and John Horgan, distinguished surgeon, have travelled from Dublin; Bill Hayes from Kilkenny; Jim Sexton, Robert Mulrooney and Mick Leahy, famous Limerick men in their own right, have braved the elements to share a memory of what has always seemed to me an extraordinarily innocent, happy youth. We talk of the table-soccer league that occupied all our time for about a year. Everyone can remember their teams, a half-century later: Tottenham for Jim, Leeds for Bill, Blackpool for me (I was a Stanley Matthews fan), and John still doesn't understand why he picked Norwich.

I finish a wonderful day with a glass of wine in a suite whose windows overlook the broad Shannon River and the illuminated St John's Castle, and wonder at it all: how did I come to this? And what did I do to deserve it?

On Monday morning, returning to the coalface, I mentioned the delay in getting off the ground at Heathrow, and immediately 'Crooky' of old Bangor town burst into verse:

Good morning Biggles,

Those grumpy old men in non-flying machines
Having turned left are not full of beans
After a couple of hours they're ready to go
But the man in the tower he keeps saying no.
On the Heathrow tarmac still they sit
Impatiently waiting to push back a bit

But what sort of hapstance brought on Limerick sobs?
Did the pilot spill coffee all over his knobs?

Just one thing, Crooky: nobody turns left at the top of the steps of an Aer Lingus flight any more . . . except the pilot.

16 *June* 2007

Wish I could have stayed in Limerick, maybe even joined Peter Houlihan in Doonbeg for a few holes, but we've been invited to the coming-out party of Sir David and Lady Carina Frost's three sons – Miles, Wilfred and George – at Arundel Castle, Sussex, this evening. We've been there once before, years ago, at the invitation of David and Carina, as Prince Andrew and Sarah Ferguson announced their engagement. Andrew arrived late that afternoon, and bounding up to his betrothed, shouted a cheery 'Hello, Sausage!', before punching her playfully on the arm.

A lovely evening, with the Frosts' sons' young friends in the majority while David and Carina's guests roll up through the castle's portals, each more famous than the last. Is there a mover or a shaker anywhere in the world that David Frost doesn't know? Angus Deayton, Gyles Brandreth and Stephen Fry make their usual dazzling contributions, and the three young men reply, a credit to their proud parents. Sir David Frost and I are about the same age, and started on television at the same time. I remember, as a tyro newsreader on Irish television, watching the young Frost burst on to the screens of Britain with *That Was The Week That Was*. He's never looked back. I wonder if he ever stands on the battlements of Arundel Castle and, just as I did yesterday from a hotel window in Limerick, says to himself: 'How did I come to this?'

18 June 2007

Here we are again, back in the old routine, with not quite such a hectic week in prospect, although Royal Ascot looms on Friday. Providing it's not washed away – we may need snorkels instead of top hats.

Yesterday in Todmorden we had not only the harbinger of the great flood with enough rain to create a new wetland for Bill Oddie and his feathered chums, but we had to contend with a power cut that knocked out the whole of the valley up to Halifax for five hours.

The upshot was near anarchy as the Post Office and banks closed because they couldn't dispense money from their magic machines. I went into my doctor's to collect a travel form to be told that I would have to make a further journey today as 'the compooters are down', according to the receptionist who was clearly unsettled from her usual Mussolini routine. But not as unsettled as she could have been as they were closed for a half-day 'development' session in the afternoon (i.e. sandwiches and words from a drug company).

Traffic lights went out, yet motorists displayed a strange courtesy and there were no accidents. No police to be seen though.

Amazing, a simple problem and three towns just ground to a halt!

*However, one person continued to work normally. The traf-
fic warden, as the parking meters were solar-powered and
despite the torrential gloom, there was enough light for them
to work and the little man went round issuing his tickets!*
Good old Britain!
Yours aye

SIR JEKYLL STOCKINGS
THIRD ARK ON THE LEFT
TODMORDEN NOW ON MERSEY

Then, in Shepton Mallett, in the middle of a downpour that
would have done credit to an Indian monsoon, two council
workmen were seen watering the town's hanging baskets. No
wonder people are confused – flaming June, as predicted by
the Met Office, has left us up to our armpits in water, and now
they've banned the old Tony Hancock ad, penned by Fay
Weldon, 'Go to work on an egg', because of its lack of dietary
correctness. So, you can have commercials that encourage you
to fill your face with sweetened cereals or buckets of battered
chicken and chips, or stuff yourself with chocolate bars or beer,
but you can't have an advertisement that says you should eat an
egg for breakfast.

And talking of breakfasts:

*Picture the scene. Self held up on M4 yesterday and running
late. So no time for brekkie and straight into a meeting.
Finally at 11.40 I'm in a leading supermarket and desperate
for some grub.*
The 'breakfast butty' looks good so I order one.
*'We stop doing those at 11.30,' says the helpful assistant. I
beg and plead but to no avail. 'Orders from head office. Can't*

be done,' says the helpful one.

Then my eye falls on the 'all-day grill'. It's more than I want really but I notice that it has all the composite parts of the breakfast buttie, all except the bread, but not to worry for I see bread and butter can be purchased separately and joy of joys, at any time of the day.

'Can I just have a sausage sandwich? Look, you do all the bits needed and all day too,' I point out with a growing confidence that becomes me well.

'No, 'snot allowed,' says the assistant. 'I can do you two sausages and bread and butter, but not a sandwich.'

So in the end that's what I have. And not a hope it seems that 'chef' might use his skills to assemble it into a sandwich for me. A plate with two sausages and four half slices of bread duly arrives.

As I make my own sarnie I muse on good old British rules and regulations coupled with our fantastic grasp of customer service. A formidable combination and no mistake.

OBADIAH GNOBEST

19 June 2007

'Make England Smoke-free'. Once more, the thinking listener ponders if the boffins aren't missing something: the workplace is smoke-free, shops are smoke-free, pubs will soon be smoke-free, ditto all public places. However, to get to a public place, you have to pass through its entrance, where you find groups of hardened wrongdoers puffing away like things possessed. Now, can passing through a smokescreen to get to a smoke-free zone be good for you? Ireland has been smoke-free for a couple of years now, and apart from the odd smoker being sent flying by a passing bus as he has a drag on the road outside the pub, the effect has been beneficial. My own experience last year, as I attended a grand function in a Dublin hotel ballroom, was that just after the coffee was served to the several hundred people there, the great room emptied, as if by magic. The lady wife and I took the hint and left as well, only to find all of our fellow diners standing in the car park in the rain. Smoking . . .

As if we don't have enough trouble with political correctness, research continually showing us things we already know, closed-circuit TV cameras and the Nanny State monitoring our every move, here comes yer man, the Pope, with a new set of Commandments. On driving . . . So, not only are we faced with a daily dice with death on the roads from drivers using their mobile phones, shaving, reading the newspaper, or applying their mascara while hurtling down the outside lane of the motorway, now they're going to be making the sign of the Cross, and saying a little prayer as well. It'll be the rosary beads next. A listener suggests that we might as well go the whole nine yards and sing a hymn:

> *O God, our help in Austins past,*
> *Our help in Fords to come,*
> *Prepare us for the 4 by 4s*
> *That do the school runs . . .*

20 June 2007

What with the wind, the rain and the barometer dropping like a stone, has anyone else noticed that since the 'scorching hot summer' predicted by the Met Office has turned into a damp squib, 'global warming' has suddenly become 'climate change'? My pet poet, Katie Mallett, has several well-chosen words for it:

> *Tomorrow's the year's longest day*
> *And in the old time-honoured way*
> *Rain falls down on sport*
> *Of every sort,*
> *And the sky is a wet-blanket grey.*

> *And festivals wallow in mud*
> *As tents float around in the flood*
> *And of course global warming*
> *Is the cause of the storming,*
> *As the summer once more is a dud.*

Another listener, Puzzled from Moffat, drives a low-emission car, heats her cottage with a wood-burning stove, has low electricity bills, no sewage nor water tax, no gas nor central heating bills, one holiday in Europe a year, and shops as cheaply as she can. After calculating her carbon footprint on the Internet, she was stunned to see that it was 'above average'. The trick is obviously to live by candlelight, grow your own food, breathe lightly, never leave the village, and run to the castle when the brigands attack.

21 June 2007

The longest day; it will always bring back memories of dear Pauly Walters: how he hated it. For Pauly it meant the beginning of the slippery slope to dark and drear winter mornings, when he rose in the dark and, at the end of the day, went home in the dark. Rising as early as he did, at quarter to five every weekday morning, he would regularly moan that the only time he saw the light of day was during a couple of weeks in May. A cheery soul at heart, he liked to act the crusty old misanthrope, with rarely a Christmas going by that he would fail to complain about 'not wintering well', and he always left buying his presents until the last minute, on Christmas Eve. Pauly told me that he once complained to a fellow member about the diminishing number of eccentrics at Mid-Herts Golf Club, only for the man to give him a sideways look and say, 'Oh, don't worry, there are still one or two about . . .'

Following a TOG's bright idea that those Chinese brickies building two new power stations a week could be the answer to our shortage of accommodation for crims, some fresh new thinking on the shortage of prison places, and the thousands of pounds it costs to keep prisoners in custody: you simply herd a couple of hundred thousand prisoners into an open field where there are little or no material comforts, no flooring, terrible food, poor sanitation, and the minimum of shelter. Prisoners are then required to stand for hours every day and hold their arms in the air for long periods. Loud, repetitive music and weak beer are used to subdue the prisoners, who become so compliant that they will even clap, scream and shout when required. In a carefully controlled experiment in the West Country last weekend, it was demonstrated that not only will people tolerate such conditions, they will thrive on them.

Yes, it's Glastonbury time again!

Mud! Mud!
Glastonbury mud
Geriatric hippies all covered in crud
Missing Dame Shirley
By going home early
With dreams rather girlie
Of a nice soapy sud.

Rain! Rain!
Wimbledon rain
Anyone would think it's that darned Spanish plain.
And poor Andy Murray
Didn't heal in a hurry.
Sue Barker must worry
She'll get Cliff again.

THE CROOKED MAN OF
OLD BANGOR TOWN

People complaining about the rain! What do they expect, with Glastonbury, followed by Wimbledon?

22 June 2007

Bit of a social weekend, one that involves new outfits, shoes and hats. Not for me, of course – I'll be wearing the same old morning suit/black tie combination. It always reminds me of a pal of mine, rising as father of the bride to comment rather tartly on the fact that all around him he could see women in stunning new outfits, while all the men were wearing suits that had to go back tomorrow . . .

We're off to Royal Ascot, as guests of the 'outlaws' – Mike and Heather Slade, Alan's father- and mother-in-law. It's been raining pretty steadily, as it has been for a couple of months now, but we bravely pick our way across the sodden lawns to the Turf Club bivouac, to join assembled Slades and Wogans for a reviving drop, before an excellent lunch, full of laughter, good food and several more drops that leave us impervious to the elements. I'd rather just remain at the table, but Mike ushers as all to the grandstand and his 'loge', a private area with seating, and cool boxes full of champagne, shrewdly located directly opposite the winning post. When Mike Slade does something, he does it right . . .

I freely admit that watching prime horse flesh gallop by is up there with ice hockey and basketball as pursuits that leave me nonplussed, particularly as none of our four-legged friends on which I have placed the hard-earned few bob has ever troubled the judge. I've been going to Royal Ascot for damned near thirty years, and have invariably lost the children's pocket money . . . It was the Clancys who invited us first, in the Seventies. We would lunch beforehand at Michael and Kathleen Clancy's lovely house in Denham, and then, a mad scramble to get to Ascot in time for the first race. We rarely made it, and I would have been just as pleased if we hadn't made it at all. I was so content over lunch. 'Leave me,' I would plead, 'someone has to finish up the raspberries and dessert wine. I promise I'll be here when you get back.' They never did, of course . . . Off we'd go to join the heaving masses, half of Ireland in the Clancy box, and Joe Kennedy singing 'They're Cutting The Corn Around Creeslough Today'. Then, back to Denham for a swim, a barbecue, more drink, and a dull throbbing behind the eyeballs as I struggled to entertain the great British public the following morning.

This year, 'Stoker' Devonshire invited me to present the prizes, and judge the prettiest filly on Saturday, but I declined the honour. One Royal Ascot a year is about my limit, and over the years I feel it has lost a lot of its glamour. The crowds are huge, and the elegance of the ladies is increasingly marred by vulgarity and drunken behaviour. Mind you, it's always been an occasion for the girls to lift up their skirts and let their hair down, carrying half-finished bottles of vodka and flower arrangements from the boxes, as they weave their way to the exits . . .

23 June 2007

The beat goes on . . . We're off to Garsington for some uplifting music, Rossini's *La Donna del Lago*, an adaptation of Scott's *The Lady of the Lake*. My friend Max Ulfane introduced me to the delights of Garsington Opera ten years ago, and I've been a supporter ever since. The Ingrams family's lovely Elizabethan house and gardens are the magical setting; it's a mini-Glyndebourne; all black ties, evening dresses, picnics and champagne. Well, this year, the graceful picture of couples strolling through the grounds before the opera is somewhat marred by the rain, and the picnics are being held in the car park, or, more strictly speaking, in the cars. People munch away at their smoked salmon, potato salads and strawberries in the dry haven of their vehicles, accompanied by the steady drumming of the rain on their roofs. A bell goes, up go the brollies and it's a mad rush for the theatre. Not that it's a theatre; the stage adjoins the house, covered by a temporary roof that also protects the audience, and the cast make their exits and entrances to and from the house and garden. It's intimate and charming, but the musical standards are as high as in any opera house in the world.

25 June 2007

It's still raining – but it's appropriate for the next couple of days, and today in particular. For today is the funeral ceremony of Sir David Hatch CBE, a great and dear friend, snatched cruelly away, in a matter of weeks, from all those who loved him.

I met him in 1967, on the day that the BBC was celebrating the birth of its squalling new infant, Radio 1. After the grand opening, which was remarkable, even for the BBC, for the lowness of its key and total lack of occasion, the new presenters broke into desultory groups; the ex-pirates – Blackburn, Everett, Peel et al – formed an admiring group around Simon Dee, then the biggest star in the firmament, who would host a special weekend show on Radio 1, but who was considered far too grand to be photographed on the steps of the Nash church with the rest of us hobbledehoys. The small band of semi-respectable broadcasters, recruited from other than the high seas – Holness, Alldis, Wogan et al – were led down to Aeolian Hall, New Bond Street, to be introduced to the Head of Light Entertainment, a man of military bearing, Con Mahoney, and his acolytes, of whom David Hatch was one. David was a star recruit to light entertainment production, trailing clouds of glory from his days as a performer with John Cleese, Graeme Garden, Tim Brooke-Taylor, Bill Oddie and the rest of the Cambridge Circus. He'd given up the roar of the greasepaint for the security of a permanent pensionable for his family – wife Ann, and children Penny, Ben and Dick. We never worked together on *Late Night Extra*, which was Light Entertainment's contribution to Radios 1 and 2, ten to midnight, Monday to Friday.

I went on to a daily radio show on 1 and 2 in the afternoon, *Late Night Extra* petered out, but by then David had made his name as a brilliant producer of comedy, with the likes of Richard Briers and David Jason, while nurturing the talents of Mel Smith and Griff Rhys-Jones. Marked down for greater things, David was promoted to Head of Light Entertainment, Manchester, where he spent some of the happiest years of his life, before they brought him back to take over the network's Light Entertainment. It was only a couple of years more, and our boy was installed as Controller, BBC Radio 2, whereupon our paths inevitably crossed, and one of my life's greatest friendships was born. Promotions followed thick and fast for this brilliant administrator – Controller, Radio 4, Managing Director, Network Radio BBC.

In all my time in radio, he was the most outstanding manager I ever met. Unlike most senior executives in the BBC, he was a constant presence in the studios, his letters of congratulation were legendary – he encouraged, he cajoled, he criticised where necessary. He was never distanced from his producers or presenters, always working on a personal level. Our relationship blossomed: happy dinners and parties at the windmill near Amersham that he, Ann and the family had lived in since their return from Manchester, great days as his guest at Twickenham, in the company of Peter Cook, Alan Coren, Clement Freud, Richard Briers, David Jason – the funniest, wittiest men I've ever met around a dining table.

One evening I invited everybody back to dinner at our place; most went home to change and collect a partner. Peter Cook simply circled the pubs of Buckinghamshire until it was time to turn up, and then fell asleep into the first course. A pity, he was the most dazzling talker I've ever met . . .

Memories of Twickenham with David: Clement Freud refusing to sign an autograph then spending ten minutes explaining why; Robert Kilroy-Silk getting in without a ticket; Richard Briers telling everybody who would listen that he was RADA-trained and a National Theatre player, and couldn't stand rugby; David Jason crouching behind me to avoid the shouts of 'Del Boy'; and the Irishman beside us in the old West Stand at an Ireland–England game, as Ireland appeared to fade, shouting 'Come on, Ireland! Be serious!' David Hatch loved that, it played straight to his sense of the ridiculous. Such memories . . . the '92 Olympics at Barcelona when Ann and Helen came and joined us – *chipirones* and Cointreau, Gaudí and the Games . . .

After a couple of years' illness, and enormous strain and pain for the Hatch family, the darling, lovely Ann passed away, and David was alone – his children all happily married. He took a world cruise; I took him to Twickenham, for it was my turn now. He threw himself into the chairmanship of the National

Consumer Council, having retired from a Birtian BBC to which he had remained loyal, but could no longer bear.

Lonely years beckoned – and then, one evening, we invited him to dinner along with other friends, and one friend in particular, Mary Clancy. Helen thought they should sit together. David thought that from that moment they should never be apart. He wasn't a man to be thwarted and Mary was swept off her feet – never easy with a Clancy, and near-impossible with such a strong-minded, successful woman. They married in Farm Street, with a sparkling reception at the Savoy, and I was best man. There I was dressed in my best, and an American woman came up to me and asked me directions to the powder room. David Hatch thought that was hilarious, as well . . .

It was a marriage made not by the Wogans, but in heaven. David and Mary were the happiest couple anyone ever knew. They travelled the world together, bought a lovely house in Camps Bay, Capetown, joined us in France for happy holidays, and David went to so many Irish 'dos' that he could have joined the cast of *Riverdance*.

Mary and David returned from a long holiday in South Africa in the middle of April. We joined them a couple of evenings later for a charity dinner, and eight weeks later, my good old friend was dead. Today we buried him, with great sadness, love and a little laughter, because merriment and joy were what David Hatch gave, and took from life. Nobody's irreplaceable, they say. They're wrong.

26 June 2007

David Hatch's funeral ceremony had so many of the great and the good, the famous, that I couldn't attempt to list them – and it's the same today, at the Guards Chapel, Birdcage Walk, for the memorial to Ian Wooldridge CBE. Ian was a fellow member of the 'Saints and Sinners' Club, a group of kindred souls who meet up for lunches and dinners, have a laugh, and try to do a bit of good along the way. He was also one of the great journalists of our age, and the setting, the speeches, the trumpets and the choir were a fitting tribute to a man who was ever straightforwardly honest, and brave. He ran before the bulls in Pamplona until he could run no more, he smoked and drank whisky to the very end. His writing was deceptively simple, like the best journalism, never overwrought, always readable, always to the point. He was a great fan of Australia and its people, particularly its indomitable cricketers, and it was only right that Richie Benaud should extol Ian's virtues. Richie finished by introducing an Australian opera singer to give us 'Waltzing Matilda'. It was fine, beautifully sung, but somehow I think Ian himself would have preferred it performed by someone who looked like a larrikin, with corks on his hat, and a banjo . . .

28 June 2007

Those of us who thought that the world as we know it had come to an end when Albert Tatlock took off his cap in the Rovers Return all those years ago have had to go back to the old drawing board, with the news that GMTV interrupted a report on the terrible, life-threatening floods in Yorkshire to transfer immediately 'over to our reporter in Los Angeles, where Paris Hilton has just been released from prison' . . . I scoffed heartily on the radio, at the mind-numbing banality of such dumb journalism, until BBC Radio 2 news reported it on the eight o'clock morning bulletin . . . and then I received an irate letter from a viewer over a programme on the television last night called *Paris*, which apparently was all about an obscure city in France, with not a 'celeb' in sight.

Rumours have abounded all morning, but my Kirkcaldy correspondent has confirmed the bad news on sporrans: if made from badger hair, they may be taxed or destroyed. And in all probability, if conservationists have their way, their owner along with them. Let us hope that our grand new Prime Minister, also, I understand, a Kirkcaldy man, has licensed his sporran, otherwise he'll have nowhere to keep his thrifty bawbees. I'm sure I heard him make mention of the fact the other day, when he said 'Let the change begin!' Although, after ten years of Gordy's custody of the public purse, 'change' is about all people have left . . . and small, at that . . . Mind you, this proposed new badger hair cull opens a whole new can of worms: is the provenance of the nation's shaving brushes now to be called into question?

And as Al Gore raises his brilliantined head to scold us all once more, a listener has tartly asked why we have to hear about the perils of carbon emissions and global warming from politicians. Wouldn't it have more credibility coming from someone who actually knows what they're talking about, such as a scientist?

30 June 2007

A listener tells me he did his bit for the good of the country last week by giving what the television ad extolling donorship calls 'blud'. After freely giving at least half an armful, he was handed a cup of orange squash. 'What's this?' he plaintively enquired. 'What about my cup of tea?' 'Oh no,' said the nurse, 'Health and Safety, you know' . . . Obviously, in his weakened state, he wasn't capable of holding a hot cup of tea, and, of course, if he'd spilt a drop on himself, the NHS knew all too well that he'd be straight on to 'Injury Lawyers For You' . . . Can something not be done about these ambulance-chasers that infest daytime and satellite television? Mind you, they're only in the ha'penny place compared to the endless opportunities offered to people in debt to 'consolidate their loans', and put themselves and their children, even to the fourth and fifth generation, in further debt . . . Delicacy appears to have gone out of the window as far as advertisers are concerned, as well. Constipation and diarrhoea we have abided these many years, but ladies who wet themselves while laughing? Little boys and lavatory smells? Softening your stools? A bridge too far, sir . . .

The brother Brian and the beauteous better half Pauline have flown the wide Irish Sea to join us this evening at Garsington for Strauss's *Ariadne Auf Naxos*. Actually, they arrived last night, and we went to Katherine and Henry's terrific gastro-pub the Greene Oak. I'm so proud of my daughter and her husband – the place hasn't had an empty table for lunch or dinner since they opened last August . . .

It's raining even harder for Strauss than it did for Rossini.

The audience is dry, but the performers, entering from the garden, are soaked by the time they get on stage, which is so slippery a nymph nearly breaks her neck. She sings on, spread-eagled, and the cast rise magnificently above the elements. *Ariadne* is silly, even by operatic standards, the classic combined with the knockabout, but it's one of the best things I've seen at Garsington in ten years.

My old pal Ken Daly introduced me to opera when we were hardly out of knee socks. His da knew somebody in the Dublin Grand Opera Society, which annually staged a festival of Italian opera, and Ken and I joined as 'supers', extras. I became a Venetian in *Othello*, a waiter in *La Traviata*, an altar boy in *Cavalleria Rusticana*, and a very pale Assyrian slave in *Aida*, because I refused to coat myself in revolting cocoa butter. Opera has changed since them good old days at the Gaiety Theatre, Dublin – acting is required now, as well as singing. Although, every so often, reality is challenged by musical needs. As in Verona last year, when the delicate Japanese, the tragic Cho-Cho San in *Madame Butterfly*, was sung by a large Italian lady in her middle years. You've just got to close your eyes, and listen to the music . . .

1 July 2007

It's still stair-rods, cats and dogs, but we're having a 'bit of a do' today. Not being eejits, we've hired a marquee, so it's a dry lunch for friends, family and neighbours. Well, everybody's dry on the outside, but well watered otherwise, and it's a splendid afternoon – good food, good wine, good company. The outlaws, the Slades, are with us, the bold Mike taking time out from racing in his frail barque around the Isle of Wight, Lord and Lady Mawhinney, such warm friends, our dear Allisses, who are going on, typically, to a charity evening in Southampton. The Smiths are here, our lovely neighbours Sir Jack and Lady Page, and Roy and Mary, who keep us supplied with rhubarb, spinach, raspberries, all the fruits of their garden. We're so lucky with our neighbours ... Brian and Pauline are still with us; there's daughter Katherine, as big as a house – only a couple of weeks before another Wogan/Cripps grandchild. She's brought our first grandchild, the darling, russet-haired Freddie, and Mark and Susan, with the wonderful Harry, a beautiful bruiser at seven months. Alan and Kate here, too, happy and loving ... The afternoon blends into evening, the last guests leave, it's ten thirty, I'm up for work in the morning. I collect two glasses of water, and make my way

Not a drop spilt

upstairs. Halfway up, I lose a shoe. I attempt to put my foot back in, and the next thing, I'm at the foot of the stairs, seeing stars. My head has banged against the bottom step, and there's blood! Various inebriated family members bring me to my feet, and attempt to staunch the flow. As I sit in the kitchen, I wonder what happened to the two glasses of water I was carrying. They were both in my hands as I fell. They're on the kitchen table, not a drop spilt from either glass. I put it down to years of training . . .

3 July 2007

It's the second week of Wimbledon, and, astoundingly, it didn't rain yesterday, for the keenly awaited rematch between a long-legged darling of the courts, Daniela Hantuchová, and the magnificent Serena Williams, who, unseeded, had wiped Maria Sharapova, the number one seed, off the court, at the Australian Open Final. Serena's performance yesterday left that in the shade of a koolibah tree. First, she gets a cramp, and immediately falls to the ground, shrieking. Why didn't she put her foot on the ground, same as you and I, when we get a cramp in bed? Don't ask. Medical help is at hand – more pain-laden shrieks, wrapping and binding. Our heroine staggers to her feet, and plays out the set in obvious agony, barely able to return a ball, but strangely, serving with her customary severity. Her completely flummoxed opponent distractedly hits the balls out, or into the net. Papa Williams shouts instructions and encouragement from the stand, then – praise the Almighty! – it rains . . . The players are out again, an hour or so later. Serena heavily bound, and limping badly. Poor soul can hardly move in between shots, but is serving like a demon, running and leaping in the air when she hits a winner. None of us has seen anything like it, least of all her bemused, intimidated opponent . . .

This morning, I happen to mention that if Serena doesn't win Wimbledon this year, she'll certainly be in line for an Oscar. A young listener tartly points out that I know as much about sports injuries as my sainted granny, but at least a couple of TOGs are with me:

> *Sir Leader, my dear old thing,*
>
> *So Doctor Who is going to have a new assistant, is he? I think they were conducting auditions yesterday at Wimbledon – and have almost certainly found the woman they seek. I cannot remember seeing such acting as that of Serena Williams as she wobbled around the court while successfully distracting her opponent. Now that was a challenge for any Dalek the BBC care to produce.*
>
> *Regards,*
>
> STEWART EGLIN
> KIRKCALDY

> *Why are you the only member of the British media to notice Serena Williams's blatant cheating yesterday? Even the good old* Telegraph *appears to have employed a blind and deaf reporter, concentrating only on Serena's notebook of motivational tips.*
>
> *Well, I have some for her opponent today, Justine Henin to jot down:*
>
> *do not get into the lead – this will bring forth a Bafta-winning injury display from your opponent;*

she saves the loudest grunts for the softest serves – but this is coincidence, not cheating;

if the game is closely poised in the third set, your opponent will develop a desperate need for the 'bathroom', which will mysteriously disappear;

don't expect sympathy from the press if she cheats – her father is vociferous and litigious – and scares PC reporters to death.

do listen to Wogan for the only honest post-match appraisal.

BEN CHEROLDBOY

I'd forgotten – Miss Williams continually asked for a comfort break before her opponent was due to serve. It was refused by the umpire, who offered her a chance to go to the bathroom before her own service. Mysteriously, on each such occasion, Serena's need seems to have disappeared . . .

Of course, I should never have told my listeners about my unfortunate accident on Sunday night:

When an injured Serena Williams battled to an incredible win over Daniela Hantuchová in the fourth round at Wimbledon on Monday, the American, suffering from extreme calf strain, dropped to the ground in pain. Went down like a sack of potatoes she did, which made me think of you. Both of you so brave. She motivated by wanting to get her hands on the trophy and you wanting to get your hands on the bottle . . . doesn't it make you feel proud.

5 July 2007

So, rum and raisin ice cream cannot be sold to youngsters because it may lead to a taste for the demon drink, leading to a life of drunken debauchery. No wonder there is panic among the sweet- and pudding-eating classes. It'll be sherry trifle next, then sticky-toffee pudding and goodbye, banoffi pie. Wine-gums will be getting the bum's rush, as well . . . Just as I was bemoaning the increasingly ridiculous strictures of our Nanny State, a letter from a listener tells of a children's party to which her little offspring had been invited. After a couple of helpings of the fruit salad, she noticed that her usually lively child was unusually placid, even soporific. In answer to her query, the hostess cheerily admitted, 'Oh, yes, I put a couple of glasses of Cointreau into the fruit salad, just to give it a bit of zing . . .'

Despite the harbingers of doom, there's still a healthy spirit of enquiry among my listeners:

> On the 7 a.m. news a news item was slipped in that will rub-bish the global warming doom-mongers, take away from the government an ideal excuse to raise taxes. That scientists have discovered that there's no chance of the ice caps melting even if the average mean world temperature increases 5 degrees above norm. No mention of it on the 7.30 or 8.00 a.m. news. No doubt the security services are on the ball. Do you think that on the midday news there'll be reports of a scientist discovered in a wood having committed suicide???
> Regards,
>
> NIGEL FISHER

On the subject of global warming, we keep hearing about these environmentalists complaining about passenger jets being a major cause of global warming. So, Boeing invent a new jet that's 20% more efficient than any of its competitors, uses less fuel, less emissions, etc. So now the environmentalists complain that the cheaper jets will lead to cheaper prices and so encourage more flights. We can't win, can we? Is it me??

PAUL

According to the Radio Times *(other listing mags etc . . .), if I stop eating beef I will be helping to save the earth, due to the fact that Daisy the cow's methane emissions are 21 times more harmful to the atmosphere than CO_2. Now if you ask me, a sensible way to cut the harmful emissions would surely be to eat Daisy, ergo no further harmful emissions.*

Just a thought. Other thoughts are available from . . .

JANET THATCARDIGAN
RACEY CHELTENHAM

Lads, lads, you might be right, but it's a little too late – the political green ball is rolling – and I'm sure we'll all grow to love those windmills . . .

7 July 2007

I don't believe it! It's Ladies' Final Day at Wimbledon, and the sun is shining! Helen and I have been invited to the Royal Box by Tim Phillips, and those decent men of the All England Tennis Club . . . The Royal Box is uncovered, like the rest of the Centre Court, while they put a roof over the hallowed turf. It'll take a couple of years, and should have been done years ago, but old ways die hard in these parts . . . A delicious lunch, in the company of Ann Jones, Virginia Wade and the Minister for Sport, then out into the heat of the day and our privileged seats to watch the culmination of two weeks of rain-interrupted attrition between the finest women tennis players in the world. The greats are there to watch it: Ann and Virginia, Billie-Jean King, Martina Navratilova, Maria Bueno and Margaret Thatcher. The French Ambassador too, because a surprise finalist is Marion Bartoli, who knocked out the favourite, Justine Henin, yesterday. It's a foregone conclusion: Venus Williams is playing her best tennis for years. There can be only one winner, and it's over in straight sets. A brave effort by the French woman . . . It'll be a lot more evenly fought tomorrow, for the Men's Final: the two greatest tennis players in the world, Federer and Nadal, at each other's throats, yet again . . .

8 July 2007

And we're there! For the past few years, our kindly pals Neil and Ann Benson have invited us to join them on Men's Final Day, and we've never had the heart to refuse . . . Every year, we assemble on the fairways of the Wimbledon Common Golf Club. Neil and Ann bring table, chairs, umbrella and all manner of sustaining provender from sushi to smoked salmon, beef to pies, tomatoes to strawberries. We weigh in with a few niggardly spoonfuls of caviar and a couple of mouthfuls of champagne. We've tucked in through wind and rain over the years, but today the sun shines yet again, unbelievably for the second day running. Is this a record for Wimbledon? No call for Sir Cliff for this year's Finals, more's the pity . . . Although I love tennis, and have played it since I was a lad, it's the same story as Royal Ascot, I'm afraid: I have the greatest difficulty pushing away the knife and fork, even to see what promises to be a great game.

Still, I unselfishly drag myself to the Centre Court for Rog and Rafa. Others to be considered, after all . . . I've been lucky enough to see most of the great confrontations of the Wimbledon Men's finals over the years: McEnroe/Connors, Borg/McEnroe, Boris Becker's extraordinary victory at seventeen; Edberg, Agassi, Ivanisevic, Sampras. Magnificent athletes, superb tennis. But I have never seen tennis like I've seen today. For sheer pace, power and excellence, it will surely never be bettered at Wimbledon, nor at any other great tennis arena. Three and a half hours we sat in the sun, and watched untouchable serves thunder down, searing passing shots skim the lines, the irretrievable impossibly returned. In the end, it was Federer's day as it has been these past few years. He retains his crown, and standing as the world's number one, but watching Nadal today, no one could ever deny his right to the titles – one day, perhaps even next year . . . Only one, little, perhaps unworthy, criticism: don't keep adjusting your underwear every time before serving, Rafa. It's not a pretty sight. Do think of the spectators, particularly those in the Royal Box . . .

10 July 2007

It wasn't all Pimm's, strawberries and cream over the weekend.

Elsewhere, other events rose and fell: the Tour de France start-
ed, with blatant disregard for geographical consideration, in
London, and then whizzed off in the general direction of
Folkestone to see if the bikers could outspeed the Eurostar.

On Saturday last, it was Al Gore's 'Live Earth'. Luckily, I
only caught the merest sensation of the great event, and a right
mess it looked. I never thought that I'd feel sorry for Jonathan
Ross . . .

*I was at Wembley on Saturday and would like you to ask the
powers that be why, after buying plastic bottles of drink in the
stadium they made me pour my drinks from the plastic bottles
into plastic cups before I could go back to my seat. Doubling
the amount of rubbish to recycle!!!*

JULIE

Meanwhile, in another part of the home for the bewildered:

*I must admit to being intrigued by a news item read out
by the news elf, Dobby Alancoat, this morning.*

*It was about the bus company, Stagecoach, running a
number of buses using sheep urine.*

How do they propose to collect it?

*Will they have a man running behind the sheep with a
bucket yelling 'Hold on – wait until I get there.'*

*Perhaps they will strap buckets underneath each sheep – or
will they be locked away in a shed for the rest of their lives?*

Regards

FRANK EVERETT
STEVENAGE

Even in far-off Ho Chi Minh City, Vietnam, it stopped a listener, John Phillips, in his tracks:

> *Did I hear the news correctly? Buses are to run on sheep's urine? Why doesn't the driver just pee in the tank when he is running low on fuel? And how did they train the sheep to pee in the tank anyway? Will the bus carry a sheep just in case they can't make it to the nearest sheepfarm?*
>
> *I've heard of cars running on Bee-Pee but sheep's urine?*

Put a sheep in your tank

CBBC Television asked me to contribute to their 'Do Something Different' campaign to stimulate the imagination of the young viewer. I've suggested that they 'smile', particularly in the face of insult, rudeness or intimidation. I've always found that it nonplusses the offender.

It even works for adults, although, faced with the kind of lunacies we have to endure on a daily basis, hysterical laughter might be more appropriate . . . And there's plenty of that on 'Wake Up To Wogan', particularly during an episode of 'Janet and John'.

12 July 2007

After years of being assured that vitamin C was a sovereign remedy and a stout defence against colds and flu, it now appears that it does as much good as your granny's red flannel and the same can now be said about the supposedly beneficial effects of fruit and vegetables as a guard against breast cancer. Then we're told that milk and cheese are good for us, and help prevent heart disease, strokes and diabetes. Men who drink 'a pinta milkaday' and regularly eat dairy products are less likely to suffer from cardiovascular disease. Hurrah! Except on the very same day that this made the headlines, a researcher at Oxford University's Department of Public Health suggested that VAT be raised on 'bad foods', such as cheese, milk and butter, to prevent deaths from – you've guessed it – cardiovascular disease . . . More tea, vicar? One lump or six? Have another dollop of cream on that scone – it won't kill you. Or will it? . . .

The strict adherence of the young to 'use-by' dates on foodstuffs defines the generations. All parents will have experienced their young adult offspring returning home to invade fridge or pantry for sustenance, only to throw out tasty tit-bits and nourishing victuals with cries of: 'Look at this! It's a day over its "use-by" date! How long did you intend to keep this in the house? You'll kill yourselves!' Yet, a listener tells me today of a recent sojourn in a caravan in Lowestoft, when her teenage son and a friend found a cake in the pantry. They tucked in with a will, kindly offering a slice to the aged parent. All parties pronounced the cake to be delicious. It was only after every last crumb had been devoured that someone looked at the 'use-by' date on the package. 'August 2006' it said . . . You can forget freezers and fridges, the answer to eternal freshness, and possibly life, lies in the hidden recesses of seaside caravans . . .

13 July 2007

It's a good job that I like opera; off to Glyndebourne, at the invitation of Michael and Lorna, to see *La Cenerentola*, a new Rossini on me. The sun is shining again, but this year, I wouldn't trust it for a picnic. Sure enough, the lawns of Glyndebourne are devoid of their customary picnic tables and rugs – a shame, as they add to the al fresco elegance of the occasion. We down a Pimm's before the bell goes, and a woman who's had a few comes up to remind me of how we danced together at a 'bit of a do', a few years ago. 'You don't remember, do ye?' It's the old cry, and it drives me to drink. For years, I used to pretend that I remembered, covering myself in confusion and embarrassment, as if somehow it was a reflection on my good manners that I had no recollection whatever of the person. And then I realised that 'You don't remember me, do ye?' was only being said to embarrass me anyway. So now, I just say 'No,' and smile, to take the curse off it . . . I could add, 'and the only reason you remember me is because you've heard me on the radio, or seen me on the telly,' but I spare them that.

La Cenerentola was blinding, and the woman sitting next to me knows where we live, and told me of her happy memories of parties in our house many years ago. She was charming. It restored my faith . . .

15 July 2007

As environmentally friendly folk, you and I are all too aware of the need to protect the planet (more of a living, breathing thing than a mere 'world'), but when there are more and more gas-guzzlers and lorries than ever on the road, more aeroplanes, more bombs, more people – is it really necessary to confine cows and sheep for long periods in order to measure the effect their flatulence is having on the ozone layer? Mark me well: the days of the baked bean are numbered . . .

Talking of 'trapped wind' – another of those television ads that are destroying the last vestiges of delicacy in British life today (anyway, surely it's 'escaped wind' that's the problem?), I was interested to hear a vegetarian on Radio 4 claim superior status to the meat-eater in the carbon footprint game, on the specious grounds that veggies don't eat cattle or sheep. Then, a further proposition, that like worthy married couples, veggies should get twenty quid a week for *not* eating meat, and, therefore, not contributing to the 250 litres of methane a day each animal emits. And what, the carnivore cries, of your bean? Hah! And think of the consequences in a confined space that can be caused by leeks, cabbage, sprouts – to name but a few odour-enhancing vegetables. The saintly Attenborough himself will attest to the constant eruptions of vegetarian animals such as the mountain gorilla. It's not the meat-eaters doing the damage, it's the meat itself . . .

16 July 2007

About midday today, daughter Katherine gave birth to Iris, a nine-pound baby girl, in St Thomas's Hospital. Hats off to my darling girl and her gem of a husband, Henry. They've successfully moved into a new house, started a new business and now brought another new life into the world. Another grandchild to be overwhelmed with clothes and toys, and, much more importantly, love. You can't have too much of that . . . Iris is our third grandchild, joining Harry, who made his burly appearance nine months ago, and Freddie, Iris's brother, who turned up, to everybody's delight, two and a half years ago.

Frankly, for a while there, Helen and I thought that our children were never going to deliver the goods, and now, well stricken as we are in years, we have the prospect of four or five of the little blighters arriving more or less at once. A delightful prospect, but as any grandparent will tell you, a wearing one. It's a good job that you have children when you're young; whenever Helen and I look after one of the grandchildren, we spend our time wondering how we coped with three young children of our own. Bev Daily, a good friend, splendid doctor, and veteran granddad, tells me that when he's playing with his grandson, exhausted, he surreptitiously looks at his watch, convinced that at least an hour has gone by, and it's only ten minutes . . .

It's strange, but whereas Helen can remember every little detail of our children's years as babies, I can remember little, or nothing. And it's not because I didn't spend time with my kids. Not having a proper job, I was at home far more than most fathers. I remember walking crying babies around at three o'clock in the morning – such things you don't forget – but my little grandchildren might almost be the first babies I've bumped into. And isn't it so much easier to change a nappy these days? And the selection of baby foods available? Delicious . . .

Tonight, it's the bright lights of the West End, and the Adelphi Theatre, for *Joseph and the Amazing Technicolor Dreamcoat*. For many years, it was my proud boast that I was the only person alive who hadn't seen the film *The Sound of Music*. Of course, I eventually succumbed, and tonight I sacrifice my prestigious standing as the only parent never to have seen *Joseph*. It's a sacrifice I'm more than prepared to make, because the saintly Andrew (Lord) Lloyd Webber has promised to donate the receipts for tonight's performance to *Children in Need*. You'll remember the great success of Andrew's search for a 'Joseph', earlier this year, on BBC TV's *Any Dream Will Do*? Well, he found his man and Lee Mead is brilliant in the role – musically and physically perfect. The show itself isn't that far from perfect, either, like a brilliantly done school play – which is how the audience received it, on their feet most of the time, cheering, swaying, singing along, as if it was their children up there on stage. A wonderfully happy evening – the culmination of a wonderfully happy day for Helen and me.

18 July 2007

A listener recounts a return trip by plane from Chicago a few weeks ago, when he noticed a fellow passenger on board struggling with hand luggage that included a baseball bat, sealed in a duty-free bag. Then another passenger got on, with a duty-free bottle of whisky. A man on the other side of the aisle had a tennis racket; then, someone else got on with another bottle of something. During the flight, several bottles were sold from the duty-free trolley . . . the thought crossed my listener's mind that if these people were terrorists he might have given them a bit of a fight, if only he hadn't been made to give up his bottle of aftershave and his nail scissors at the security check . . .

Another listener today browsing through the tangled undergrowth of the BBC website, with its tales of terrorism, global warming and the race to build another Noah's ark, came across the story of that new, huge, jumbo aeroplane. At the beginning of the repeat, the BBC put what it regarded as the most important question to us: 'Boeing unveils a new jet, the only big commercial aircraft made more of carbon fibre than aluminium. But, is it more environmentally friendly?' For heaven's sake! The important question is: is it safe? Next, how many hours will it take to get on and off the thing? To get through security? And how many weeks before your luggage turns up? Do you remember that eejit last year who said that the biggest threat to us all was not terrorism, but global warming? Are we *ever* going to get our priorities right?

19 July 2007

Parlous times indeed, for the BBC. A couple of days ago, they infuriate Her Majesty, by fiddling about with a documentary that falsely makes it appear that the Queen stormed out of a photo session. The Queen is not amused, but the newspapers are delighted, and several rainforests are given up to censorious editorials and articles. Then, just as the dust begins to settle, another scandal gets the self-righteous knockers wound up. And the BBC itself, of course. Nobody, or nothing, gets the wind up like the BBC ... It appears that there have been deceptions in phone-in competitions, not only as previously discovered, on *Blue Peter*, but horror! on *Comic Relief* and *Children in Need*! The newspapers really go to town this time, caring not a jot the damage their hyperventilated spewing might do to two charities that have raised millions for underprivileged children, both at home and in Africa. Ever since the Kelly case, the BBC has been paranoid about compliance, transparency and generally behaving as if it were Caesar's wife. The baby gets thrown out with the bathwater. All phone-in quizzes bite the dust. Ken Bruce, whose 'Pop-Master' quiz has been a major feature of his Radio 2 show for years, and beyond reproach, gets his innocence besmirched with the same brush. The TOGs get on the bandwagon:

> *Oh boy are you in trouble now! I saw the DG on News 24 yesterday claiming he wants to put an end to the deceit and deception that is apparently rife through the BBC.*
>
> *So – that's an end to people with silly pseudonyms writing from places that don't exist about things that never happened. An end to the belief that Bobby can play the organ, that Deadly drinks like a fish and that Fran never imprisons fine young men in her understairs cupboard.*
>
> *All that you'll have left is the music, a lot of dead air and your fireworks display!!*
>
> *Yours still believing*

MEGAN

So, nice to see the BBC owning up to stuff about radio and television all being faked.

Now I hear they are about to point out that the Flowerpot Men weren't Flowerpot Men, that Match of the Day *is actually a collection of Subbuteo men filmed from a distance, Sue Lawley never really existed, there were Three Ronnies, Huw Edwards is Scottish,* My Family *isn't really funny,* Monty Python *didn't have a flying circus, Stuart Hall is a figment of a very warped imagination,* Triangle *was written by Bill Shakespeare and 'Wake Up To Wogan' doesn't have any listeners.*

There, that should keep the solicitors from the door for a while.

Blimey, next they'll be telling me Superman can't fly, Gordon Ramsay doesn't swear and Fran Godfrey's voice is dubbed by an angel.

Oh, and don't get me started on that Santa Claus chap.

LEN HORRIDGE

P.S. The answer to your phone quiz is . . .

Useless to point out that, in the case of *Children in Need*, the storm in a teacup happened a couple of years ago, during the BBC Scotland opt-out from the main programme, when an over-enthusiastic young producer tried to help a flagging phone quiz along, by supplying a fictitious winner. It need never have come to light, if it weren't for the innate honesty and decency of the BBC. Unfortunately, there are people out there who don't have the same standards . . .

20 *July* 2007

I like to think that I have been at least partly responsible for the success of BBC2's *Rome*, by pronouncing it 'disgusting'. Viewing figures immediately rocketed; there's nothing the plain people of Britain like better than the disgusting:

> *Yesterday on your programme you read out the tale of the history teacher who wrote to parents recommending that pupils should be encouraged to watch* Rome *on BBC2 in order to aid their appreciation of classical Roman history. This reminded me of when I was a young TYG, wrestling with the intricacies of Latin at school (very handy for meeting all those ancient Romans around in adult life of course). One day my dear mother suggested that I should be allowed to stay up past my normal bedtime, in order to watch the film* Up Pompeii, *starring the late Frankie Howerd, as it would help my classical Latin studies. I did watch it and, although it did not benefit my knowledge of the language, it taught me a thing or two about conjugations.*
>
> *Carpe diem and all that,*
>
> LEIL SONWHEELS

I'm off – two weeks in a darkened room, recharging my drained batteries. All I'm getting is dog's abuse, as if I were deserting a nation in its hour of need. How welcome the still small voice of the discerning James Burton Stewart of Reading:

> *Just a line to wish you* bon vacances *as you head off on your peregrinations, leaving the tiller in the capable hands of your*

fellow honour holder and autobiography writer Johnny Walker, confirming that the show is indeed by Royal Appointment.

It's always good to go away sure in the knowledge that good things are going on in your absence – this year you are in the shortlist for the National Television Awards, according to the Eurovision Song Contest website. 'Terry Wogan is nominated for "Most Entertainment Presenter". Major, as they say. No doubt you will be, as reporters are wont to say these days, 'returning back' – hopefully at the ceremony there won't be an 'outage' to stop the 'revolve' working as happened the other evening at the great first night. We can't have you ending up 'sat there sitting' – that would be too big 'an ask'.

Bon voyage.

Epilogue

Just before I sign off, and apply myself to the grouting and rendering, heartening news: the brave TOGs who have raised millions for *Children in Need* with the TOGs calendar and by giving countless hours of unpaid, unsung time to selling, posting and packing *Janet and John*, and *Janet and John Reloaded*, tell me that they've just received a cheque for nearly £300,000 from the Treasury, returning the VAT claimed on the sales of 'Janet and John'. The Treasury say that it's a 'one-off' gesture, brought about by the pressure of public opinion, and the hundreds of TOGs letters to the government, and their MPs. 'One-off?' We'll see about that, when they try to charge VAT on *Janet and John Reloaded*, which is flying out the doors of TOG helpers, even as we speak. *Janet and John* raised £1.1 million by last November's big night. With the VAT, it must be pushing another half-million by now, and *Reloaded* will do even better, or I'm no Old Geezer. On the night of *Children in Need* last year, a record-breaking £18 million was raised in seven hours of live television. We've just distributed £33 million to Britain's children who need it most. That's about £400 million in twenty-eight years. And people ask me how I can stand getting up at half five every morning. Because you're worth it . . .

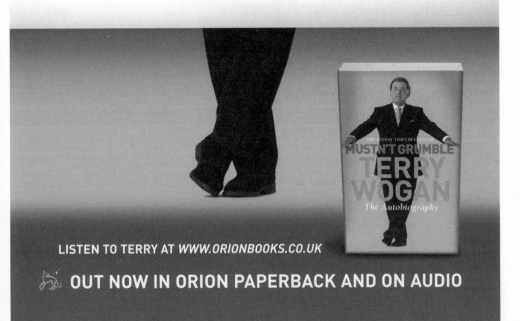